Small Claims Court in Ireland
A Consumer's Guide

Damian McHugh, B.L.

Foreword by

Judge Mary Collins

Judge of the District Court

This book was typeset by Artwerk Ltd., Dublin
and printed by Johnswood Press, Dublin

Published in 2003 by First Law Limited
Merchant's Court
Merchants Quay
Dublin 8
Ireland
www.firstlaw.ie

© First Law Limited

ISBN 1-904480-07-1

A catalogue record for this book
is available from the British Library.

This book is dedicated to the memory of the late
Joe Christle, formerly of the College of Commerce,
Rathmines, Dublin, for his vision and initiative in
making it possible for many mature students, like
the author, to qualify as a barrister-at-law

CONTENTS

Foreword xi
Preface xiii
Introduction xix

Chapter 1: The Small Claims Procedure 1
    The Rules 1
    Processing a Claim 3
    Recommendation 5
    Administration of the Scheme 5
    Settling Claims 6

Chapter 2: How Civil Claims Are Judged 8
    The Courts 9
    The Trial 9
    The Judge 11
    Small Claims Court 12
    One Big Difference 13

Chapter 3: How To Bring A Claim 15
    Consumer's Rights 15
    Communication 17
    Pre-Condition 17
    Consumer's Duty 17
    Entering the Small Claims Process 18
    How to Start 21

Chapter 4: What Happens After a Claim is Filed and Admitted? 24
    Setting Out the Claim 25
    The Options the Respondent Has 26
    What Happens if the Respondent Admits the Claim? 27
    Where the Respondent Consents to Judgment 28
    Understanding the Language 28
    Paying By Instalments 29

Chapter 5: Disputing A Claim.............................. 31
   Getting the Parties Together.............................. 32
   When the Respondent Does Not Reply 33
   Set-Aside 36
   Appeal.. 38

Chapter 6: The Court Hearing.............................. 39
   Preparation... 40
   Witnesses 41
   Guidelines.. 42
   When the Case is Called.................................. 43
   The Evidence... 44
   The Judgment 45

Chapter 7: The Sheriff.................................... 47
   If the Respondent Fails to Pay Up 48
   No Goods... 49
   The Practice.. 50
   County Wicklow... 51

Chapter 8: Chasing The Debtor By Other Means...... 52
   Instalment Order 52
   Examination Under Oath 53
   Prison 55
   Other Methods of Enforcing Payment...................... 56
   Deterrent... 57

Chapter 9: An EU Initiative For Small Claims 58
   Existing Small Claims Procedures in Member States 60
   Monetary Limits in Each Sate............................. 61
   Introduction of the Procedure............................ 62
   No Obligation to Engage A Lawyer......................... 62
   Assistance 62
   Alternative Dispute Resolution 63
   Relaxing the Rules Of Evidence 63
   Costs.. 64
   Appeals 64
   Questions 65

Chapter 10: Case Histories 66
  Case Against a Jewellery Shop 66
  Rent Deposit Case 68
  Second Rent Deposit Case 71
  Lost Baggage 72
  Defective Car 72
  Another Claim Against a Garage 73

Chapter 11: Statistics 75
  Holiday Claims 75
  Rent Deposits 76
  Furniture 77
  Other Claims Received 77
  Claims Dealt With 78
  The Year To March 2003: Dublin 78
  Outside Dublin 80

Appendices
  Appendix A: Legal Words And Terms Explained . 83
  Appendix B: Forms 86
    Form 53A:1: Application to Small Claims
    Registrar 86
    Form 53A.2: Notice of Claim Against
    Respondent 91
    Form 53A.3: Notice of Acceptance of Liability . 92
    Form 53A.4: Notice of Dispute of Claim 93
  **Appendix C: List Of District Court
  Office Addresses** 94
  **Appendix D: Small Claims Court Sittings
  in 2003** 105

Index 106

FOREWORD

Damian McHugh's book on The Small Claims Court is a timely and informative book on the alternative procedure of commencing and dealing with a civil proceeding in respect of a small claim.

The Small Claims Court was fully established as part of The District Court in 1993 following a two year pilot. It was set up to meet the need of the ordinary man or woman to seek redress through the court in small civil cases without the fear of incurring costs if they lost. The Small Claims Procedure provides speedy, cheap and relatively easy access to the Courts.

This extremely helpful book takes the reader through the various steps in bringing a claim from the initial contact with the Registrar, through the court hearing itself to the procedure for recovery of monies on foot of the judgment where the respondent defaults. It highlights the important role played by the Registrar in facilitating the settlement of a high proportion of claims. The chapters on case histories and statistics are particularly interesting.

Damian McHugh's journalistic background, his vast experience as a Court reporter, combined with his legal background as a practising barrister, ensures the reader gains a clear understanding of the court system and procedures within the context of the Small Claims. The book is presented in clear language and the provision of case histories together with the author's own observations of the conduct of cases in the Court makes it a comprehensive and interesting guide. As the title implies it is aimed at the consumer but undoubtedly it will be of great interest to students and legal practitioners, consumers associations and citizens' advice groups. Mr McHugh is to be congratulated on producing such an invaluable resource.

Judge Mary Collins
District Court
May 2003

PREFACE

This is not a law book. It is a book about the law or more specifically a book about one small but very important aspect of the administration of justice. It is a book about a court, the Small Claims Court and the small claims procedure. It might also be called 'The People's Court,' as it is often referred to, especially in the United States where the services of the court are widely availed of. Most of all, *The Small Claims Court in Ireland: A Consumer's Guide* is a book written for ordinary men and women with no knowledge of the workings of this court and the procedures associated with it. The book strives to throw light on an aspect of the administration of justice which does not receive the media attention it deserves.

When I set out to research this book I knew little of the court, other than there was such a court in this country. Nor did I know that the EU Commission had issued a Green Paper this year designed to encourage wide-ranging consultation on possible measures that could be introduced throughout Europe to, among other things, simplify and speed-up small claims. By pure coincidence, publication of this book coincides with the closing date for receipt by the Civil Law Reform Division of the Department of Justice and the Commission of observations and submissions by the public and interested parties on the proposals in the Green Paper.

The EU is trying to ensure that individuals and businesses are not prevented or discouraged from exercising their rights "by the incompatibility or complexity of the legal and judicial systems in the member states." One thing that emerged clearly from the limited research carried out for this book was that no such obstacle exists here. On the contrary, the small claims procedure has been streamlined into a model that could, with some changes, be recommended for every other EU State. Nonetheless, it could be improved upon and made more attractive to the general public in a number of ways, reference to which are made elsewhere.

On one occasion that we chose to visit the Small Claims Court in Dublin, there were no lawyers present to defend claims. On a second occasion, a barrister and a solicitor were engaged to defend a particular claim for their oil company client. One budget airline always uses a solicitor to defend claims. That is their prerogative but it is also inherently unfair to lay people who are expected to handle their cases competently, faced with a professional lawyer in the opposite corner. This is an issue raised in the Introduction to this book and is something that lends itself to reform, if not by the Oireachtas then by the EU.

A second way in which an exclusive small claims procedure could be made more attractive for the ordinary citizen to use would be by setting aside particular days for the court to sit throughout provincial Ireland. At present, only the main urban areas have such exclusive sittings. If that were done, the relative informality of the sittings would possibly be more widely availed of by the general public as a forum to redress perceived consumer injustices.

Thirdly, the Small Claims Court receives very little publicity in the popular media. Only when word leaks out that a particularly interesting case is due for hearing – such as a recent claim brought by a woman arising out of a liposuction procedure – will reporters be assigned to the court. Perhaps more could be done to encourage the media to report these court proceedings. By doing so, the media would be getting stories and copy of good public appeal and human interest and, at the same time, it would hopefully encourage the public to use the court and the accompanying procedure. The more it is used, the more successful it will become.

Small Claims Court in Ireland: A Consumer's Guide sets out to reach the same audience as the predecessor to this book, *Going to Court: A Consumer's Guide* – the general public, those people who know little, if anything, about the courts themselves, where they are located or how they work. Not just the Small Claims Court itself but also the system which backs up the court, the main focus of which is to negotiate a settlement between the parties to a particular claim, something that is not generally known or accepted. That is the particular value and attractiveness of this court system above all others. The primary role of the officials who operate the small claims procedure is to affect a compromise between the opposing parties. Sometimes this works, sometimes it does not and when the latter is the case, the dispute will find its way into the court list for adjudication by a judge.

The book also includes samples of the forms that must be used in order to bring a claim or to defend a claim. In addition, it contains a comprehensive list of the Small Claims Courts throughout the country together with the name of the chief clerk attached to each and other helpful information.

The Small Claims Court in Ireland is written with the intention of explaining the mechanics or procedures and also the operation of the small claims procedure for ordinary citizens and to give them a preview or insight into the offices which back up the court and especially into the court itself. Hopefully, it provides helpful information and advice, not just on how a claim is brought and fought but how a person who brings a successful claim goes about collecting his or her money from the unsuccessful respondent.

It is this latter point that perhaps needs more attention. While most parties who defend claims are reputable and pay up on the decree granted against them by the judge of the Small Claims Court, others are not. They will do everything they can to frustrate a person trying to enforce a decree, by changing address if need be, and it is not unusual for the bailiff to return empty handed after several visits and warnings to some operating under the guise of reputable business concerns. While the EU is trying to tackle this problem at Community level, the hope is that it will have a knock-on effect domestically so that the system does not fail at the last hurdle the very people it is designed to help.

The system can only get better and become more consumer friendly. This will especially be the case when the small claims procedure becomes a fully-integrated on-line service. While forms can be downloaded on the Courts Service web site (www.courts.ie), they then have to be at personally handed in to the small claims offices. Work is being undertaken on the system, which will enable a person to complete and submit the claim on-line and to pay the €9 fee in similar fashion. This is part of the multi-million Euro e-courts initiative designed to modernise the courts service and to allow the public to conduct business electronically with State bodies.

Once again, I want to express my grateful thanks to my wife, Claire for not alone her help in producing this *petit opus* but for putting up with my long periods of absences in doing so. Very special thanks are due to the staff of the Courts Service generally but especially to the head of its information service, Helen Priestly, to Eamon Doherty, Marion Roarty and Anne Marie James, small claims registrars attached to the small claims office in Dublin for their invaluable help throughout, to Jim Aherne of the Circuit and District Court Directorate for broadening the scope of this book to encapsulate EU development in the area of small claims and to Alan Donnellan, chief clerk in the District Court office in Bray for producing very worthwhile statistics in the court area that he is responsible for. Special thanks for also due to two members of the Judiciary who sit on the bench of the Small Claims Court from time to time whom I encountered along the way and got helpful advice from – Judge Mary Collins who graciously responded to my request to look through the manuscript and to write the Foreword for this book, and to

Judge Michael Connellan for the insight he provided for me into the working of the court on a recent memorable day.

My grateful appreciation goes also to the Dublin County Sheriff, John Fitzpatrick for unselfishly providing of his time to inform me of the work he and his staff do to enforce decrees granted by the small claims court, and to Mary C. Joy in the Civil Law Reform Division of the Department of Justice for comprehensively updating me on developments at European level which could have a future effect on our small claims system.

Last but by no means list I want to express thanks to Thérèse Carrick for her work in editing this book and to Bart D. Daly, Managing Director of First Law Ltd, publishers of *Small Claims Court*, for his work and vision in creating this series for the benefit of the public as consumers of the courts generally and, in this case, the Small Claims Court.

Damian McHugh
May 2003

INTRODUCTION

I attended a sitting of the Small Claims Court in Dublin earlier this year for the purpose of experiencing at first hand how the court operates in practice. Although the Court has been in existence for more than a decade, it was the first time I had seen it in operation. The reason for this is that practising barristers such as myself would never be briefed to attend the court and represent a client, whether for the plaintiff (who is known as the claimant in the Small Claims Court) or for the defendant (who is known as the respondent).

My understanding also was that solicitors would not normally attend either. The basis of this erroneous belief was that the Small Claims Court was designed to handle consumer claims cheaply without the involvement of a solicitor, much less a barrister.

That is the theory and that is the practice, by and large, but to my surprise on the very day I chose to visit District Court No.54 in the Richmond Buildings, off Church Street, just five minutes walk from the Four Courts, where the Small Claims Court judge presides from time to time, a barrister was present to represent a respondent and, in compliance with the code of ethics of the Bar, was attended by a solicitor.

On the other side of the case, a young woman with a claim of €1,100.00, which is very close to the upper limit of compensation or damages that the court has power to award, stood alone, and very much held her own, against the two professional lawyers, a type of David and Goliath situation. She was treated with courtesy but was not guided by the District Court judge who was very conscious of the apparent unevenness of the contest unfolding before her.

Later in the hearing, a solicitor 'friend' of the claimant announced his appearance for his client who, he said, felt intimidated by the lawyers pitted against her in what was intended to be a hearing conducted without the involvement of lawyers. After hearing arguments on behalf of both sides, the judge found largely for the claimant and suggested that the parties should get an estimate for the damage, which she found the respondent responsible for. Some time later, the barrister returned and handed a piece of paper to the Court Clerk. The judge was informed that the respondent would pay €700 to the claimant on the basis of the judge's finding on liability or fault.

In a way, this case is a cameo of what the Small Claims Court is all about. While the appearance of a barrister in this court and the expertise she brought to the forum represents an exception to the rule, as it were, it nonetheless did not present an insuperable obstacle to the young woman, who 'won the day' before her solicitor friend arrived and made submissions on her behalf. She was not put at any disadvantage by the appearance of lawyers acting for the party she brought her claim against. The judge saw to that and that is the beauty of the Small Claims Court and the Small Claims Procedure which is available to every man and woman in this country who as a consumer buys goods or services for private use from someone selling them in the course of business.

There is nothing to stop a claimant or a respondent from engaging the services of a solicitor or barrister to represent them in the Small Claims Court but if they do, they will be responsible for the lawyer's professional fees, even if they win. The court does not grant costs to the successful party. Lawyers don't come cheap and it would be a pyrric victory indeed if the claimant was awarded the maximum €1,269.74 and then have to pay that amount and perhaps more to their lawyer.

It's arguable that the limit of €1,269.74 (i.e. the equivalent of £1,000 in old money) should be increased. For example, in Northern Ireland, the limit is Sterling

£2,000. The average in most States in North America is $5,000 although in one State, at least, it is $15,000. In England, claims of up to Sterling £5,000 are heard as a small claim although the limit is £1,000 for certain claims including, notably, personal injury which are barred from the small claims procedure in this country.

That limit of £5,000 in England was set in 1999, the same year that the monetary limit for claims under the small claims procedure was increased here from £600 following a review.

A Commission currently examining the power or jurisdiction of the various courts, may well recommend increasing the power of the District and Circuit Courts to award greater sums that the maximum they can now award, €6,348.69 in the case of the District Court and €38,092.14 in the case of the Circuit Court. If those limits are increased in the near future, a strong case could then be made out to give the Small Claims Court power to award amounts up to a maximum of, say, €2,500 from the current unwieldy figure. This would significantly increase the attractiveness of the procedure to consumers by making access to the courts' system virtually free. The only cost in most cases would be the newly increased fee of €9.

In the chapters that follow we will endeavour to explain what is involved in taking a claim through the Small Claims Procedure and, hopefully, throw more light on what is a valuable weapon in the growing armoury of Irish consumers.

CHAPTER 1

THE SMALL CLAIMS PROCEDURE

THE RULES

The small claims procedure came into operation in this country on December 10, 1991. The rules under which it operated were the District Court Rules (Small Claims Procedure) Rules 1991 (S.I. No. 310 of 1991). Originally, it was run as a pilot scheme. It proved successful and since then has been growing in popularity as an alternative method of commencing and dealing with a civil proceeding for small claims, i.e. claims with a lower value in monetary terms than those usually handled by the District Court. It was, and is, known as the Small Claims Procedure.

It is very important to understand from the outset that the entire scheme applies only to consumers in a very definite sense. According to the rules a "consumer" is a purchaser of goods or a service of a type ordinarily supplied for private use or consumption, where the purchaser does not make the contract in the course of a business and the vendor (the seller) does make the contract in the course of a business.

Also, the person who brings a claim is called 'the claimant' and the party against whom the claim is made is called 'the respondent.'

The early rules described a "small claim" as any civil proceeding instituted by a consumer against the vendor in relation to any goods or services purchased in which the amount of the claim due could not exceed £500. In addition, the claim could not arise from an agreement under the Hire Purchase Acts 1946 and 1960, or from an alleged breach of a leasing agreement.

There was a minor change to the rules brought about by the District Court (Small Claims Procedure) Rules 1992

(S.I. No 119 of 1992), introduced on May 29, 1992, which empowered the Small Claims Registrar or designated District Court clerk to take affidavits (sworn statements) or affirmations in claims processed through the small claims procedure.

More substantial changes were introduced by a new set of rules in 1993. The District Court (Small Claims Procedure) Rules, 1993 (S.I. No. 356 of 1993) extended the definition of 'small claims.' Under the new definition, claims brought by consumers include minor damage caused to the property of the claimant.

Although torts (civil wrongs) were included from December 8, 1993, when the new rules took effect, a claimant could not claim damages for personal injuries caused by the tort of negligence in this country. That is also the case in Northern Ireland and in England under their small claims procedure, although not in some States in the United States of America where it is possible to claim such damages. The 1993 rules expressly exclude personal injuries. The claimant cannot be a body corporate, i.e. a company.

We can therefore say with certainty that a person who suffers minor injuries in a road accident, at work or in a fall caused through the negligence of others, such as on the public road following recent repair or remedial works, are barred from bringing a claim for damages in the Small Claims Court.

The 1993 rules also introduced a further heading under which a claim can be taken through the small claims procedure. This related to tenancies. A tenant who has a claim against his or her landlord in respect of the non-return of the rent deposit or any sum of money known as "key money," may take the case through the small claims procedure. Again, the claimant cannot be a body corporate.

The limit on claims since the inception of the scheme was £500 but that was increased to £600 in the District

Court (Small Claims Procedure) Rules (S.I. No. 377 of 1995), which came into operation on January 22, 1996. The limit remained at £600 for a further three years.

The District Court (Small Claims Procedure) Rules 1999, which came into force on July 1, 1999, raised the upper limit to £1,000. This translates into €1,269.74, the limit that exists today. The Rules of 1993 and 1995 were annulled by the 1999 Rules.

At this stage, it should be emphasised that the small claims are read in conjunction with all the other District Court rules in force. This is provided for in the 1999 Rules themselves and is something that is very much in favour of a claimant, as we shall see, trying to enforce a decree for a sum of money against an unsuccessful respondent who is unwilling, or refuses, to pay the decree to the claimant.

PROCESSING A CLAIM

The *Guide* to small claims, produced by the Courts Service, states that the small claims is an alternative method of commencing and dealing with a civil proceeding in respect of a small claim and is provided for under the rules, as we have shown above. It is a service provided to the public through their local District Court office, anywhere in the country.

Although the scheme is designed to handle consumer claims cheaply, without involving a solicitor, in practice a claimant can turn up in court for the hearing of their claim by the District Court judge and be confronted, without any advance notice, by a respondent who is represented by a solicitor. This has happened to many claimants since the scheme came into operation.

While due process and constitutional justice allows any party to a court action to be professionally represented, not alone by a solicitor but by a barrister also where the circumstances warrant it, surely it is against the spirit of the small claims procedure for a claimant especially to arrive in court and have to prosecute their claim in the face of a party supported by an individual who has a wealth of legal knowledge and experience.

This can be traumatic and off-putting for the person, even though the judge would ensure that the hearing would be conducted in as fair a manner as possible. But even in that situation it could be argued that the scales of justice are not being held in an even fashion.

The vast majority of small claims are processed through the Dublin District Court which sits once or twice every two weeks in the comfortable surroundings of the refurbished Court No. 54 in the Richmond Building complex on Brunswick Street, near the King's Inn on the aptly named Constitution Hill and also quite near the Bus Átha Cliath depot at Broadstone. Days are specifically set aside for the hearing of small claims in that court and little, if any, other business is transacted during the hours devoted to the small claims. The only people present usually are those directly involved in the small claims cases.

That, however, is not the situation in all District Court venues throughout the country where small claims' business is transacted. Usually a number of cases – as little as one or two – are slotted into a District Court sitting which is especially devoted to hearing civil claims on a particular day. However, at other venues, a number of small claims can be scheduled into a sitting in which there are civil and criminal cases listed for hearing. Claimants have arrived at these latter sittings and had their cases taken up for hearing at the start of the day's list of cases in courtrooms packed with lawyers, witnesses, individuals appearing on criminal charges as well as members of the public generally, and only then have they learned that the party opposite is represented by a solicitor. In those circumstances it is not difficult to understand, and to sympathise with such a claimant's view, that they felt intimidated and were unable to do justice to their case, no matter how helpful the judge might be.

RECOMMENDATION

It is strongly recommended in the interest of fair procedures that where a party to a small claim engages a solicitor to represent them in court, that notice to that effect be served on the other party, at least seven days before the date fixed for the hearing. This notice would allow the other party to consider engaging a solicitor, or at least obtaining legal advice, in advance of the hearing.

A rule could be introduced by way of a statutory instrument, which would make it mandatory on parties to small claims to notify the District Court Clerk of the particular area in which the case is being taken of the fact that they will be professionally represented at the hearing. In that event, the Clerk would serve notice of this fact on the other party, the claimant or the respondent, as the case may be. As a consequence, the claimant, or the respondent, if that is the case, would not be caught by surprise on the day.

ADMINISTRATION OF THE SCHEME

Quite simply, every District Court in Ireland is a small claims court and the District Court Clerk for a particular court district is the person charged with responsibility for administering or processing small claims taken in a particular district. He or she is known as the Small Claims Registrar who is a central, indeed crucial, figure in the administration of the entire scheme in a particular district. Elsewhere, (see Appendix C) a comprehensive list of every District Court in the country together with addresses, the name of the Chief Clerk for each district, the telephone and fax numbers and the office hours are provided.

The entire ethos of the scheme is to give consumers a means of bringing on claims in an inexpensive way without recourse to the courts. In effect, it is a simple claims procedure within the District Court. What is lost sight of is the fact that it is not designed to go to court at all. It is principally designed to have a claim by a consumer dealt with in a room. It is a facility in which the two opposing parties can have the issue between them mediated by a District Court Clerk who is called the Small Claims Registrar for the purpose of administering the scheme.

The success of the scheme depends on how effective the Registrar is in performing the duties and functions associated with the scheme. While District Court Clerks for the most part have many other functions to perform in connection with the 'normal' court lists, as it were, those Clerks who act as Registrars of the small claims procedure in Dublin are so busy in handling a growing number of claims coming into their offices that they are involved full-time with administration.

SETTLING CLAIMS

The primary function of the Registrar is to try to settle the case. Where possible, the Registrar will negotiate a settlement without the necessity of a court hearing at all. Only when he or she has been unable to settle the issue in controversy between the parties, will the case be listed for hearing before the court. In other words, only where the parties fail to agree on terms, will the Registrar be left with no alternative but to refer the matter to the court.

The Registrar is not a judge and therefore cannot administer justice. Although, having said that, if a difficult claim is successfully negotiated by a Registrar, the claimant will walk away feeling that the Registrar has dispensed justice. However, it has to be acknowledged that only a judge appointed under the Constitution, has the power to administer justice in the constitutional sense.

Once again, it must be stressed in this context that the Small Claims Court is the District Court. It is not a separate court called the Small Claims Court. It is the District Court hearing civil cases and as part of its remit it deals with cases with an upper limit of €1,269.74. It is a court like any other court and which, in the not too distant future, may be the subject of a European-wide standard for civil and small claims under proposals, which are currently under consideration by officials in Ireland and other EU Member States.

In the next chapter we will look generally at how civil claims are judged.

CHAPTER 2

HOW CIVIL CLAIMS ARE JUDGED

Viewers of the popular American TV courtroom programme, *Judge Judy*, the Small Claims Court judge, will know that she has the power or jurisdiction to award sums of damages or compensation up to a limit of $5,000. They will also see how she arrives at her decisions, because, like most judges, she explains the factors that influenced her, whether it is on a point of law or perhaps, where there was a conflict on the evidence given by the parties on opposites sides, simply on what party she believes.

Like or hate the aggressive manner in which she operates her court, it is compulsive viewing for many people who identify with the role of *Judge Judy*, to such an extent that it gives them 'a feel' for the court and a yearning, perhaps, to become a player themselves in some capacity, if not as the judge who displays much common sense in making her rulings which, it should be noted, "are final." We shall see in later chapters in this book that the decisions of our Small Claims Court differ in many respects from that of *Judge Judy*, not least because here there is a right of appeal for both parties to a claim.

When this writer was deciding whether to embark on a course of study that would lead to qualification as a barrister, he took advice from several sources, not least from a very senior member of the judiciary. The statement he made to me that day still resonates today. "Law," he said, " is 75 per cent common sense, and 25 per cent rules." Believing that I had the necessary mental equipment to cope with the common sense requirement and that with a sufficient burning of the midnight oil to learn the 25 per cent of rules I might make it, qualification followed five years later.

Even though there was still a huge amount of post-qualification learning to follow, the common sense element is still the ingredient that is most essential in deciding whether to take a claim, not just as a consumer in the small claims procedure but as a plaintiff in any form of civil action in the courts of this country.

THE COURTS

Going back to first principles, we should first understand a few very important things about the courts. The Constitution of 1937, which is our fundamental law, provides that justice shall be administered in public in courts established by law by judges appointed by the President on the advice of the Government. It also states that these courts shall consist of Courts of First Instance and a Court of Final Appeal, to be known as the Supreme Court.

The Constitution states that the Courts of First Instance shall include a High Court with full original jurisdiction (i.e. power to commence hearings of any type) and courts with local and limited jurisdiction. These are the District Court and the Circuit Court, which were established by legislation and are run by rules. The Small Claims Court is the District Court but with a lower ceiling on the amount of money it can award as a decree. The following puts the power of each court in perspective:

- High Court: It has power to award unlimited damages i.e. it has no ceiling.
- Circuit Court: It can award damages up to a maximum of €38,092.14.
- District Court: Limit is €6,348.69.
- Small Claims Court: The judges can award sums up to a limit of €1,269.74.

THE TRIAL

Civil claims, whether in the District Court, the Circuit Court or the High Court are run in an adversarial fashion.

The person or party bringing the claim is on one side of the court. The opponent is on the other. Each party is represented by a solicitor in the District Court, and by a solicitor and barrister in the Circuit Court. In the High Court, the parties will each be represented by a solicitor, a barrister and a senior counsel, perhaps by two senior counsel.

The idea behind the Small Claims Court is that there should not be lawyers in attendance, even though there is no bar to them appearing and representing the claimant or the respondent.

The case is run as the lawyers in their professional opinion feel it should be. They may call their client into the witness box to give evidence, to set out the facts as only they know how because it is their individual case and only they know how the problem or the case develop from their own perspective. When the client has finished giving direct evidence or evidence-in-chief as it is known, the client will usually be questioned, or cross-examined on the evidence that has been given, by the lawyer representing the opposing party. That can be a traumatic experience for any person. The prospect of this cross-examination is very often the reason that people settle or even withdraw their claim.

However, that should never be a reason or excuse to bring the curtain down on a claim. The lawyer must use the skills at his disposal to bring the judge around to find in favour of his client. One of these skills is the use of language and the ability, through training and experience, to undermine the evidence given to the court by a member of the opposing side, whether it is the plaintiff or claimant or the defendant or respondent and, also, to look for inconsistencies in the witness's evidence. If a person is giving truthful evidence to a court, he has nothing to hide. No amount of intense cross-examination or play on words by a silky-tongued lawyer can change that.

In fact, the more that a lawyer presses such a truthful witness, the more it usually becomes clear that the lawyer is clutching at straws and hoping the witness weakens. It takes a strong character to stand up to such intense cross-examination but one very positive thing that people should take from it is a resolve not to let the opposing lawyer 'get the better' of them in such circumstances. That, unfortunately for some, is not the end of the matter because tactics and advocacy skills rather than finding where the truth lies often win the case.

Using tactics, the lawyer might decide not to call the client to give evidence. However, that is extremely unlikely in a civil case although it is common in criminal trials for a variety of reasons that do not concern us here. The lawyer may also decide to call witnesses whose evidence supports that of the party bringing the claim or that of the party defending the claim. These witnesses may be expert in a particular field, such as a doctor, an engineer, an architect, an actuary, a motor assessor, a health and safety consultant or an occupational therapist.

THE JUDGE

The judge may decide to ask questions of one or all of the witness or of the principal parties themselves while they are in the witness box. They could also be recalled to the witness box long after they have concluded their evidence. The reason for this is that some relevant matter, which the judge feels is important to the issue that has to be decided between the parties, needs further amplification or closer scrutiny as a result of the evidence that has already been given to the court.

Other than that, the judge rarely intervenes in the conduct of a trial. At least that is the situation in most courts, but not the Small Claims Court. The judge is the sole arbiter of not only the law but also of the facts presented in the course of a civil claim. One of the very few exceptions to this statement is the trial of a defamation action in the High Court in which the jury decided all issues of fact.

Judges are very good observers of everything that happens in their respect court. They watch and they listen. They ask questions and they take notes. They draw inferences from evidence they have heard and they reach conclusions. Faced with two witnesses who are putting their own 'spin' on the same set of facts and are therefore in total conflict with each other, the judge will test the veracity of the evidence and draw his own conclusions. He will decide which of them is the more credible, in other words whose evidence will he believe.

This is one of the main reasons why respective courts are slow to set aside the findings of a judge who hears and sees witnesses and makes decisions based on how he perceives that witness. It is a question of credibility, which is of the essence in trying to establish the truth in any given case. Appeal court judges do not hear or see witnesses. Apart from the legal submissions, all they have to assist them is a transcript of the evidence, a book of questions and answers, which do not show the demeanour of a witness or the reaction of a witness under cross-examination.

SMALL CLAIMS COURT

The judge who presides over the Small Claims Court in any of the courts around the country is no less a judge than the judge who presides in the District Court, in the Circuit Court, the High Court or in the Supreme Court. He or she is a District Court judge appointed by the President on the advice of the Government who made and subscribed to the declaration required under Article 34 of the Constitution to execute his/her office as a judge of the District Court "without fear or favour, affection or ill-will towards any man" and to uphold the Constitution and the laws.

The reason this is emphasised is that the Small Claims Court is often perceived as being something less than a court administered by a kind of junior judge. To believe this is to ignore reality. The court is very much a court in the true sense, in which a duly appointed judge tries to administer justice between the claimant and the respondent.

There is no panel of specially appointed persons who sit as judges from time to time in the Small Claims Court. The judges who sit on these courts are chosen from time to time from other work in the District Court. For example, Judge X may be sitting in one of the District Courts in the Bridewell at the rear of the Four Courts in Dublin today and tomorrow may be sitting in the Small Claims Court in the Richmond Building in nearby Brunswick Street.

The judge sitting on the bench in the Small Claims Court brings a wealth of experience to a different arena. This includes all the skill and knowledge at his or her disposal, including observing and listening to the parties and their witnesses, if any, drawing inferences from evidence, coming to conclusions and establishing the credibility of the various parties who give evidence to the court. Like any other judge in any other court, the Small Claims Court judge for the time being will apply not only common sense but also the legal rules and principles appropriate to the facts and circumstances of the particular case. Every case is decided on its own merits or facts.

ONE BIG DIFFERENCE

Anybody who has been present in the Small Claims Court in any one of the many venues throughout the country will note one big difference from other civil courts. That is the conciliatory nature of the proceedings in which the judge will try to bring about a resolution of the issue between both parties. In fact, even before the claim ever reached the court, the District Court Clerk, who is the Small Claims

Registrar, will have tried to negotiate a settlement without a need for a court hearing at all. Only if the Registrar has been unable to bring about a settlement will the case be listed for hearing. This is the theme under which Small Claims Procedure operates and it is the focus of the chapters that follow.

In Chapter 3 we will examine the different types of claim that can be dealt with by the Small Claims Court and show how members of the public should go about bringing a claim.

HOW TO BRING A CLAIM

CONSUMER'S RIGHTS

When a person goes into a shop and buys goods, they have a contract with the shop, the seller. Even though the word 'contract' is never mentioned between the customer and the seller and even though nothing is reduced to writing to support the existence of a formal written contract, the law implies the existence of one and that is very important, not just for the customer but also for the seller. That unspoken contract, as it were, is just as tangible as the one written on a sheet of paper with the name of the seller printed on the letterhead.

Under that contract the customer who bought a washing machine, a computer or a lawnmower, for example, is entitled to expect that the washing machine will wash clothes, that the computer will do what it is supposed to do and that the lawnmower will cut grass. The law deems or implies certain representations to have been made by the seller, unless such representations are expressly excluded by the terms of the bargain or contract. A customer is entitled to expect that:

- An item of goods that cannot be used for its normal purpose is not of merchantable quality because according to the applicable law, the goods should be of merchantable quality.

- The goods should also be fit for their intended purpose, that is, the normal purpose that such goods are used for or for some special or particular purpose that was made known to the customer when buying the goods.

- The goods should be as described, whether that description is written on the goods or was represented by the seller at the time of purchase, and

- The goods should correspond with the sample, if they are buying goods by sample.

All four expectations are rights which consumers have when purchasing goods. After taking possession of the goods it may turn out that they are faulty. In normal circumstances, the buyer will return to the shop where the goods were purchased, make a complaint and expect to get satisfaction. Why is the shop the first port of call in this situation? The reason is that in almost every case the seller is the party responsible for putting things right, for ensuring that the washing machine, the computer and the lawnmower do what they are supposed to do. Essentially, as we have shown above, the retailer is the party to the contract with the customer and must perform his side of the bargain, which are his obligations under the contract.

It is not the function of this book to advise as to the law in any particular area. Rather is it intended as a guide for members of the public who would like to know about the small claims procedure and how to go about bringing a claim through the procedure and then to the Small Claims Court should attempts at negotiating a settlement between the parties fail. In any event, while setting out briefly some of the rights consumers enjoy when they purchase goods, it is appropriate also to outline some rights enjoyed by consumers when they pay for a service. As with the purchase of goods from a retailer, a contract exists also between the customer and the person providing the service. Therefore, we can say that a customer as consumer is entitled to expect:

- That the supplier has the necessary skill to provide the service,
- That he or she will provide the service with proper care and diligence,
- That materials used will be sound, and
- That the goods supplied, if any, as part of the service will be of merchantable quality.

COMMUNICATION

A District Court judge who frequently sits in the Small Claims Court told the writer: "If people communicated, there would be no Small Claims Court. There would be no need for it."

The consumer who ended up with faulty goods or who received an abysmal service should immediately make contact with the seller of the goods or supplier of the service, as the case may be. They, in turn, have an obligation to put matters right for the consumer. They cannot run away from their obligations. The parties in the first instance must communicate with each other to try and rectify the problem to the satisfaction of the consumer once the complaint is genuine. Communication is a first principle and should normally lead to a successful solution or conclusion from the consumer's point of view.

PRE-CONDITION

In all these situations, the goods or services must be bought for private use from somebody selling them in the course of business. That is an absolute pre-condition to a claim by a consumer being accepted for processing under the small claims procedure.

CONSUMER'S DUTY

Consumers have duties to perform also. Although the advice that follows should more properly be included as part of the court hearing itself, it is being mentioned here for the purpose of putting potential claimants on notice at an early stage. They have a duty to mitigate their own loss. That is a fundamental principle of contract law. In practice, it could mean that the customer who purchased the defective lawnmower was obliged to return it to the shop as soon as possible and in the state in which it was purchased. It does not mean that just because it was damaged or faulty that the purchaser should delay reporting the loss or damage by leaving the machine outdoors in the elements where it was allowed to deteriorate.

ENTERING THE SMALL CLAIMS PROCESS

When the consumer fails to get any satisfaction from the seller, whether in that situation the complaint is ignored or the consumer is fobbed off with excuses such as being told to take the matter up with the manufacturer of the particular goods, for example, their remedy is to take the seller of the goods or provider of the service, whatever the case might be, to court.

It is a big step to embark on litigation, at any level, and one that should not be taken lightly. That is very much the situation with respect to the Small Claims Court because a person bringing a claim is not intended to be professionally represented by a solicitor and must therefore be prepared to go-it-alone. If they want to engage a solicitor to represent them, they may do so but they must bear in mind that if they win or loose, they will be responsible for the lawyer's fees – simply because the court has no power to grant costs to the successful party.

Apart from the costs' consideration, a number of other factors should be considered by a person before seeking out the clerk of the particular District Court to start the small claims process:

- The consumer must be satisfied that the goods or services were bought from somebody selling or providing them in the course of business. The procedure is not available for use by one businessperson against another.

- That the claim is for money, a monetary amount of damages, and that it is no more than €1,269.74. It can be for what is known as a liquidated claim, one which has a fixed amount of money attached to it, or an unliquidated claim, one which has an estimated amount of money attached. The latter is the more common form of claim, covering damage caused to property or for repairs as a result of damage caused or for faulty workmanship. The small claims office will decide under what head the claim should fall.

- That the claim is not for a hire-purchase agreement.
- That the claim is not for a breach of a leasing agreement.
- That the claim is not for a debt.
- That the respondent – if it is a company or corporation – did not go into liquidation since the goods were purchased. If it did, it would almost certainly be a fruitless exercise to try and recover a decree.
- They should have done their homework on the party against whom a claim will be made to establish exactly who the respondent is or should be. Is it an individual? Is it a sole trader? Is it a company? People have to be prepared to look behind the façade, the name over the door, to see whom exactly the named respondent will be. It is more difficult to enforce a decree against a fly-by-night cowboy passing himself off as a carpenter, plumber, house repairman or other tradesman than against high street traders generally. However, the sheriff can also testify to having difficulty trying to enforce decrees against so-called highly reputable multi-national retail business houses.
- Is there a witness who can be relied on to give evidence in order to support the claim being made?

As we mentioned above the person contemplating bringing a claim should first try to get satisfaction by using the direct route, by making direct contact with the shop, office or other party. The normal form of communication is the personal contact but when that fails, people will, and should, resort to making contact by letter. Too often, business people ignore complaints on the basis that the customer will forget it and go away. They should remember that Irish consumers are much more enlightened today about their rights and are less likely to walk away unsatisfied than heretofore.

If a consumer fails to get the problem rectified by calling or by telephoning, they should write a letter, outlining the basis of the complaint and set out what exactly is being claimed. The letter could be drafted as follows:

> 21 Market Street,
> Glenealy,
> Co. Wicklow.
> 29 March, 2003

Dear Sir,

On the 4th February this year I bought a roll of carpet in your shop and paid €900 for it. The carpet was delivered to my home two days later and when the carpet-layer came to put it down on the hallway he took the plastic wrapping off the roll of carpet, unrolled it only to discover that the pattern in the middle of the carpet was badly faded.

It was obviously defective and should not have been sold as top wool carpet.

I have called in to your shop and I have also telephoned on numerous occasions without ever getting to speak to the man who sold me the carpet or to any person willing to speak to me or to take responsibility. Your receptionist has taken my name and number but nobody has made contact with me.

Your firm is responsible for the carpet that you sold me and I expect to hear from you without further delay.

Yours faithfully,
XXX

If there is no response or no adequate response to the letter, a further letter should be sent to the firm in roughly the following terms:

21 Market Street,
Glenealy,
Co. Wicklow.
11 April, 2003

Dear Sir,

I refer to my letter to you dated 29 March, 2003 regarding the carpet I purchased from you and which was found to be badly faded when it was opened.

Nobody has contacted me from your firm and unless I hear from you within 14 days from the date of this letter I will bring a claim against you in the small claims court to recover the cost of the carpet, €900.

Yours faithfully,
XXX

Receipts for the goods purchased, delivery docket, copies of the letters and any other documentation that the customer has in connection with the purchase should be safely kept because they will be needed to process the claim. The letter(s) written and any other evidence of contact with the shop, such as an itemised telephone account showing the number of calls made to the shop or firm by the customer, are also extremely important. They are evidence to show attempts to have the problem rectified before the court claim was commenced. Essentially, they show that the customer acted as reasonably as possible and only embarked on the small claims procedure as a last resort. This evidence will weigh heavily with the judge should the case go all the way to a hearing.

HOW TO START

Personal contact should be made with the Small Claims Registrar at the particular office relevant to the claim. This is not always easy to establish. If, for example, a Tralee-based person is taking a claim against an airline for baggage lost on route between Shannon and London, the claim should be taken in the court area in which the airline has its registered office, even though the person boarded the flight at Shannon Airport, Co. Clare. The claim should therefore be taken in the Dublin Metropolitan District and the relevant small claims office in that district that the person should visit or contact is located in Áras Uí Dhálaigh, beside the Four Courts in Dublin 7.

Details of the location of local District Court offices are available at the back of this book in Appendix C. They are also available on the Courts Service website (www.courts.ie), in the Eircom telephone directory under the Courts Service entry in the Green pages section. Information is also available from the Citizens' Information Centres and the Office of the Director of Consumer Affairs, 4-5 Harcourt Street, Dublin 2 (tel.01-4025555; Lo-Call service 1890-220 229) or at their Cork office at Norwich Union House, 89-90, South Mall, Cork (tel. 021-427 4099).

When contact is made with the relevant local District Court office, the Small Claims Registrar or a staff member will provide the person with a special application form. This form can be downloaded from the Courts Service website. However, as the service is not yet fully automated, it is not possible to complete and return the form via the Internet.

The fee that has to be paid for making a claim is €9. This was set, along with many other District Court fees by the District Court (Fees) Order 2003 (S.I. No. 87 of 2003), which came into effect on March 10, 2003. It increased the cost of instituting a small claim from €7 (£6). When the small claims procedure began more than a decade ago, the fee was £5 so, despite the two increases since then, the fee remains small and consumer-friendly.

The application form may be completed under guidance from the staff in the office and when this is done, the form and the fee are lodged with the Small Claims Registrar in that office. The original of the completed application form is retained in the office and a copy is sent by the Registrar to the party against whom the claim is being taken. From here on that person or party will be known as the respondent while the person bringing the claim, formerly the customer, will then be called the claimant. A whole new experience is about to unfold for that person.

In Chapter 4, we will look at what happens next.

WHAT HAPPENS AFTER A CLAIM IS FILED AND ADMITTED?

The form that the claimant fills out the form that is used to commence proceedings is Form 53A.1 (see **Appendix B**) which must be lodged with the Small Claims Registrar together with the €9 fee. The Registrar and the District Court office staff members will assist the claimant to complete the form, if help is needed, and it usually is.

It cannot be stressed strongly enough or repeated too often that the claimant must exercise great care when submitting the name of the respondent. Accuracy is extremely important because the claim could fail if the wrong party is named as the respondent. If the respondent is an individual, his or her full name and address should be entered on the form. If the respondent is a limited or public limited company (Ltd or plc), the full name of the company, including the 'Ltd' or 'plc', must be entered together with the full postal address of the company's registered office.

If a claimant has just a general idea that the respondent is a company but does not know how to go about checking the proper name or registered office of the company, the information may be obtained at the Companies Registration Office, Parnell House, 14 Parnell Square, Dublin 1 (tel.01-804 5400; Lo-Call 1890 2220 224; website www.cro.ie).

According to the rules, the Small Claims Registrar must record in the Small Claims Register the name of the address of both the claimant and the respondent, the date of the application, the nature of the claim and any other relevant details in relation to the claim. At that stage, the

Registrar is obliged by rule 4 of the Small Claims Procedure to "consider" the application and is then given absolute discretion to take such steps as he deems necessary to record the full facts of the claim, whether by way of interviewing the claimant or otherwise.

This, of course, is done in the District Court office. If it should transpire that the claim does not come within the scope of the small claims procedure, the claimant will be informed and the fee, if it has been paid at that stage, will be refunded. As we have shown, the rules do not allow claims arising under a hire-purchase agreement, a breach of a leasing agreement or for debt. A claim for damages for minor personal injuries would also be outside the scope of the procedure as would a host of other types of claim, including claims for libel or slander and, of course, claims where the amount of damages exceed €1,269.74.

SETTING OUT THE CLAIM

Setting out details of the claim should not be too difficult. The facts of the case should be written in a simple and clear way, rather like a short essay. Things that you might focus on are:

- How did the claim arise?
- Whether the claim was related to goods purchased, services provided, to minor damage to property or for the non-return of a rent deposit.
- If the claim is related to purchased goods, when and where they were bought, their cost, the identity, if known, of the person who sold them on behalf of the vendor.
- Detail the particular circumstances of the particular transaction
- What the problem was.

If the Registrar considers that the claim is proper or appropriate to be taken under the Small Claims Procedure, he must serve a notice of claim on the respondent by registered post. This notice is Form 53A.2 (see **Appendix B**) which will be accompanied by a copy of the claim contained in Form 53A.1. Two other forms will be sent to the respondent at the same time. These are Forms 53A.3 and 53A.4. (see **Appendix B**).

OPTIONS OF THE RESPONDENT

One of the forms sent to the respondent offers a number of choices or alternatives that can be followed, depending on the attitude being adopted. Of course, the option that the respondent takes will be dictated by the particular circumstances of the individual case. In a good many, if not all, cases, a respondent will view a claim as a nuisance and may decide at a very early stage that it would cost more time and trouble to defend or dispute the case than it was worth.

However, before looking at these options in more detail, the content and purpose of these forms is explained as follows:

- Form 53A.1 is a notice of application to the Small Claims Registrar in which the claimant sets out his or her name and address, the name and address of the respondent, particulars of the claim and signs and dates it. The purpose of the form is to enable the applicant to apply to have the claim processed through the small claims procedure in accordance with the provisions of the rules.

- Form 53A.2 contains the actual notice of claim against the respondent with the names and addresses of both parties to the claim, particulars of the claim, dated and signed. It offers a number of options:

  (a) It advises the respondent to whom it is addressed that if he admits the claimant's claim, he should complete and detach Form 53A.3 and return it to the Small Claims Registrar within 15 days of receipt of the notice.

(b) It also advises him that if he wishes to dispute the claim, he should complete and detach Form 53A.4 and return it to the Registrar within 15 days of receipt of the notice.

(c) The third option is for the respondent to discuss the claim with the Registrar, again within the same 15-day time frame.

(d) Fourthly, it advises the respondent that if he does nothing about the notice, he will be held to have admitted the claim and the claimant could proceed to obtain judgment against him without further notice to him.

WHAT HAPPENS IF THE RESPONDENT ADMITS THE CLAIM?

We will try and explain this in more detail. If the respondent admits the claim after receiving notice of it from the Registrar, and

(a) agrees to pay the amount claimed, or

(b) consents to judgment being given against him, or

(c) wishes to pay the amount claimed by instalments,

he must complete and return the Notice of Acceptance of Liability (Form 53A.3) to the Registrar within 15 days of receiving the notice and claim. That is the ideal situation for the claimant who will be informed of this outcome by the Registrar.

Where the respondent agrees to pay the full amount that has been claimed by the claimant, he may send it directly to the Registrar, along with Form 53A.3 (Notice of Acceptance of Liability). Cheque, postal order or money order are the accepted forms of payment. When payment is received by the Registrar, it will then be sent to the claimant.

If the respondent's agreement to pay is conditional, e.g. on condition that the goods are returned by the claimant, the Registrar will inform the claimant of this and seek his or her agreement to comply with the respondent's requirement.

WHERE THE RESPONDENT CONSENTS TO THE JUDGMENT

Sometimes, respondents notify the District Court office that they are consenting to the judgment being given against them. Where this happens, the Registrar puts a procedure in train that culminates with the court entering judgment for the decree against the respondent. This is provided for under the rules. It involves the claimant applying for judgment. This is done by the claimant swearing what is known as an affidavit of debt (i.e. a sworn statement), setting out briefly details of the claim and the consent to judgment in the amount of the decree by the respondent. The Registrar will help the claimant to draft the affidavit and with the procedure involved. When completed, the affidavit is lodged with the Registrar along with a requisition for judgment and a small claims decree.

UNDERSTANDING THE LANGUAGE

Having been involved in various capacities with members of the public as litigants, lawyers and judges, courts and the courts' personnel throughout one's working life, one of the biggest bug-bears voiced by the public was the language used by lawyers and judges in court. Words and phrases that roll off the tongue of lawyers, almost as their first language, are extremely off-putting for people who have no prior involvement with the law or the courts. To them it seems that lawyers, including their own advisors, are deliberately speaking 'above their heads' to give them an air of superiority and to show how knowledgeable they are in the complex field of law, in much the same way as doctors and other professionals are often accused of the same behaviour.

Lawyers do not as a rule knowingly speak in the presence of clients in this fashion. However, it is possible that they to do so without realising it. They should, of course, be conscious of this and realise that it is very much in their interest as well as the client's to have their client as fully informed as possible so that they are not left 'in the dark' with respect to what is being said and what is happening around them. Only in this way will they be able to acquit themselves with credit.

If a party, who is a claimant or a respondent in the small claims procedure, comes across words, phrases, legal terms or language generally that they do not understand and are used in their presence, they should ask the user to explain it, whether it was uttered by a judge, a lawyer or a court official.

The reason this issue is raised at this point is because of the use of the word 'affidavit' under the previous sub-heading. One has to constantly remind oneself that the language of the lawyer is not the language of the general public. In addition, the impact of the complex legal language, if not the meaning itself, will be totally unknown, and may lead to misunderstandings and misconceptions or other difficulties, if it's not properly interpreted and explained.

While the lay person will not usually come into contact with lawyers in the course of their progress through the small claims procedure, in some cases they will. In those situations they should be conscious of their right to be kept fully informed. Having stated all of this, people will find that the Registrar and District Court staff generally are extremely helpful and will do everything possible to smooth the passage of the case through the procedure for the claimant and the respondent - without using complex legal language in the process.

PAYING BY INSTALMENTS

Sometimes a respondent will require time in which to pay the amount due. There is absolutely nothing wrong with such a request. In fact, many claims are disposed of in this way. Rule 6 of the District Court (Small Claims Procedure) Rules makes provision for this eventuality. It states that:

- Where the respondent wishes to pay the amount claimed by instalments, the Registrar shall seek the consent of the claimant to the terms proposed by the respondent.

- The details of every agreement reached or settlement effected under this rule shall be recorded in the Small Claims Register.

It can be seen from this that the claimant will not only be kept fully informed by the court staff of the fact that the respondent wishes to pay the amount of the claim by way of instalments, but the claimant has the right to give his or her consent to such an arrangement. While the rule makes no reference to the fact that the claimant may refuse to give consent, any liberal interpretation of the rule would imply such a meaning to it.

In this regard, it is of interest to note that when the framers were drafting these rules they envisaged that interpretation of its contents might arise from time to time. For that reason, the provisions of the Interpretation Act 1938, which is used in courts at every level to help interpret primary and secondary legislation such as Acts of the Oireachtas and Statutory Instruments are also applicable to the small claims rules.

In Chapter 5 we will look at what happens when a respondent disputes a claim.

CHAPTER 5

DISPUTING A CLAIM

One of the big benefits of the Small Claims Procedure is that if the respondent admits the claim against him and agrees to pay the amount claimed, or consents to judgment being given against him, or wishes to pay the amount claimed by instalments, the claimant will not have to attend court at all. It becomes a painless exercise for the claimant, without having to suffer any of the trauma normally associated with going to court. However, a court appearance will become inevitable if the respondent fails to pay the money after admitting the claim and exercising one of the three options.

Very few respondents opt to pay the money by instalments. In the considerable experience of one Small Claims Registrar, there was only one respondent who chose to pay the claimant in that way. In that particular case, the respondent agreed with court staff that he would pay the money by direct debit to the claimant's bank account. In accordance with the rules, the claimant was asked if she would consent to this manner of payment, and agreed. But the respondent reneged and, as a consequence, the matter was brought to the court by the Registrar where judgment was entered against him for the full amount of the claim. He was forced to pay the decree in one sum.

In any event, court staff prefer if unsuccessful respondents and claimants against whom a successful counterclaim was brought by a respondent, discharge their liabilities in one full payment. In the case just outlined, the respondent's refusal to pay by instalments as agreed was treated as a disputed claim and was taken to court for a hearing by the Small Claims Registrar on that basis after getting the claimant's consent to do so.

It is reasonable for parties who appear as respondents in small claims proceedings to question what length of time they will be allowed in which to pay the sum of money owing to either the court staff or to the claimant directly. The normal period within which respondents are expected to pay is two weeks. If the money is to be paid directly to the claimant in that time frame and is not, then the claimant should notify the Registrar immediately of this. Should that happen, the court staff will bring pressure to bear on the respondent to settle up. The threat of being taken to court usually results in prompt payment.

GETTING THE PARTIES TOGETHER

The whole basis of the small claims procedure is to get the parties to settle the matter and not to have to resort to court at all. That is the mission statement of small claims and one that is not readily understood. Every effort is made to get the parties to a dispute to arrive at a satisfactory conclusion and, in order to facilitate that objective, District Court staff will act as mediators.

Sometimes, the Registrar will call the respective parties to a meeting in an office at the particular District Court relevant to the area in which the claim is being taken. Such conciliation meetings are conducted in total privacy with the Registrar acting as the negotiator. The particular rule (rule 8(1) of the 1999 Rules) governing this situation states that:

- The Small Claims Registrar shall use his best endeavours to settle the dispute between the parties and in that connection may interview the parties any other person whom either party may wish to hear. Where a settlement is effected, particulars thereof shall be recorded in the Small Claims Register.

While the rules makes it mandatory for the Registrar to use his best efforts to bring about a settlement, he is given absolute discretion by the rule in deciding in the first place whether and how he will interview the claimant and the respondent and also any other party that either the claimant or the respondent might wish him to interview. It can, therefore, be seen that the Registrar is not obliged to bring the parties together for a settlement meeting. However, he must still do his best to bring about a settlement.

In practice, the respective parties are usually interviewed over the telephone by the Registrar in a conciliatory attempt to get them to agree terms. These efforts are usually successful and it is only when the Registrar fails in this objective that the case finishes up in court before a judge. If such a meeting of the parties is arranged, the Registrar will ask both parties to outline the facts of their respective case and may question either or both of them in an effort to clarify the issues.

If an agreement cannot be reached, the Registrar must set about arranging to have the matter brought to court. He has no option but to do this under the rules. He may therefore there and then fix a date, time and location for a hearing of the claim before a judge of the Small Claims Court. These details will be posted to the parties before the date fixed for the hearing.

WHEN THE RESPONDENT DOES NOT REPLY

It would not be unusual for respondents to ignore claims submitted to them by the Small Claims Registrar. If the respondent fails to return either the Notice of Acceptance of Liability (Form 53A.3) or the Notice of Dispute (Form 53A.4) to the Registrar within 15 days of service of the Notice of Claim and the copy of the claim on him, and fails to contact the Registrar within that period of time, he will be held to have admitted the claim. A respondent who chooses to ignores the notice served on him by the Registrar is doing himself or his case no favours.

When a respondent fails to reply, the procedure that

will be adopted is the same as that provided for in the rules where a respondent consents to judgment, that is, by way of rule 11. This rule provides that in such a situation the claimant may then apply to the court for judgment in the amount of the claim. The matter then proceeds in the following way:

- The claimant swears an affidavit of debt. He or she will get assistance from the Small Claims Registrar and court staff in putting the claim together and swearing to the fact that what has been written in the sworn statement is the truth (That is the essence of an affidavit, as we have shown in the previous chapter).

- The affidavit of debt is then lodged with the Registrar. Also filed with the Registrar at the same time is a requisition by the claimant for judgment and a small claims decree.

- The Registrar will then proceed to judgment in the same way as if the Notice of Claim and the copy of the claim were a civil summons issued and served under the District Court Rules, 1997. The applicable orders under these rules are Orders 39 and 45.

For the purpose of completeness, these Orders are explained as follows:

- Order 39 deals with the commencement of civil proceedings in the District Court, including all matters relating to the issue and service of civil summonses, a description of the parties, the defence, costs, the time periods allowed and so on.

- Order 45 deals with the procedure where the plaintiff/claimant can get a decree made in his favour in circumstances where the defendant/respondent ignores or chooses not to defend the claim. This is known as the judgment in default procedure, a procedure which is also widely used in the Circuit Court and High Court. (As we shall see later, it is possible for such a defendant/respondent to go to the court and give reasons why the court should vary or set-aside the order granting the decree (see p. 36).

The other order from the 1997 District Courts Rules concerning small claims is Order 46.

- Order 46 is concerned with the hearing of civil proceedings. This provides for such matters as the absolute discretion of a judge to grant a decree or to grant a dismissal on the merits or without prejudice to the right of the plaintiff/claimant to proceed by way of a new civil summons. It also deals with situations where the defendant/respondent brings a claim against a plaintiff/claimant. This is known as a counterclaim and the order provides that it may be heard as a separate action. Also covered by the order are situations where the parties to the action do not appear in court on the date fixed for the hearing of the claim and, perhaps, counterclaim.

Going back to the case on hand where the respondent fails to reply to the claim, the claim will be listed for determination by the court. As to when the matter will be listed for hearing depends very much on the number of civil cases awaiting their turn to appear in the court list for the particular court area. However, when the case is listed before the relevant Small Claims Court, the judge will enter judgment for the amount claimed and grant the decree. There can be no dispute or controversy about the claim for the simple reason that the respondent has chosen to ignore the claim and it will, therefore, be treated as an uncontested claim.

Similarly, if the respondent had put in a counterclaim against the claimant after being served with the original claim, and then ignored the entire procedure by failing to respond to telephone calls, letters and other forms of communication from court staff, the claimant would proceed to get judgment in the manner just described. In addition, the judge would dismiss the respondent's counterclaim. That illustrates the folly of the respondent who might have had a very valid claim against the claimant.

The Registrar will follow the exact same procedure in getting judgment entered against a respondent and a decree made where the respondent reaches an agreement or settlement and then defaults on the agreement or settlement.

SET-ASIDE

For many people, especially the farming community, the heading on this part of the chapter might have a different meaning, one more appropriate to how land is or is not cultivated. However, it has a special meaning for parties against whom a judgment has been entered and a decree made by a judge of the District Court or, for that matter, by a judge of the Circuit Court, the High Court or by the Master of the High Court, all of whom have power to give judgment in default against parties who, for example, ignore proceedings validly served on them.

Set-aside can arise in the following way. After the Small Claims Court enters judgment in default against such a respondent, notice of the court judgment is served on the respondent. He may or may not be shocked by receipt of this notice. If he has chosen to ignore the claim originally served on him, it is unlikely that he will be shocked but if, as sometimes happens, because of the vagaries of the postal service the claim did not arrive at the proper address, or because of some other problem such as the matter not being brought to the attention of the proper person authorised to handle such matters in a firm or company despite the registered letter being received by a subordinate in the office or perhaps the letter got mislaid, there will be shock and dismay.

In those circumstances, the respondent may bring the matter to the attention of the Registrar and hence to the court itself. He has the power under the Rules to refer any application or proceedings under the small claims procedure to the District Court for hearing. He can do this on his own initiative or at the request of either of the parties to a claim. Therefore, if a respondent claims he did not receive the original application or did not receive it in time to make a reply or for any other reason, it is up to the respondent to make such a case to the judge in court and to satisfy the judge that there was good and sufficient reason to set aside the decree. However, the respondent must convince the judge of the genuineness of his case to succeed in such an application.

His application to have the decree set-aside will be listed like any other case and the claimant, who will have been notified of the application by the Registrar, is entitled to attend and to address the court in the normal way.

One such application decided by the Small Claims Court recently concerned a claim by a householder against a large Dublin retailer over alleged defective floor covering. The claim was ignored by the retailer, and judgment and a decree for the full amount of the claim was subsequently granted by the judge of the Small Claims Court. When the retailer was served with notice of the judgment and decree, the relevant manager in the shop protested that he had not been made aware of the original claim, which, he said, was mislaid. He was able to satisfy the judge of this.

The judge in her wisdom listened to both parties. She told the respondent's representative that she would let the matter stand, meaning she was giving the parties an opportunity to try and negotiate a settlement. However, she also advised the respondent that she was prepared to allow the claimant her expenses for attending the hearing on both days after the claimant explained how she had to forgo certain money by having to attend court on both occasions.

The parties withdrew from the court and some time later, the representative of the respondent informed the court that they had agreed terms under which a payment would be made to the claimant. He also apologised for wasting the court's time. The judge adjourned the case for mention to a later date to ensure that the payment was made and, if it was, she indicated that she would set aside the decree on that day as if this was a pre-judgment settlement. Neither party would have to attend the court on the day fixed for the case to be mentioned if the settlement terms had been implemented.

This case serves as a good example of the conciliatory way in which the court operates. On some occasions, an application to set aside a judgment and decree can be treated as a hearing of the claim itself after the set-aside application is successful.

APPEAL

Despite the existence of a procedure to enable a respondent to apply to have the decree set-aside by the court that granted the decree in the first place, an alternative procedure available to such a respondent would be to bring an appeal against the order of the court to the relevant Circuit Court, the next highest court in the hierarchy of courts. However, the whole idea of the Small Claims procedure is to resolve matters at District Court level rather than by way of appeal to the Circuit Court.

CHAPTER 6

THE COURT HEARING

The heading which first presented itself for inclusion at the top of this chapter was 'The Trial' but to use that heading, with all the implications that that title conveys, would be to misrepresent what transpires – or should transpire – when a small claims dispute between two parties comes before a judge of the District Court for determination.

According to the scheme of the small claims system, the procedure and the court hearing are supposed to be informal and usually are. However, the manner in which a small claim is run and adjudicated will depend very much on the particular court venue, and whether the courtroom is being exclusively used to hear small claims on any given day. For, as was pointed out at the commencement of this book, if a claimant who is not professionally represented, turns up in the District Court for the hearing of a claim and is confronted by a courtroom packed with people awaiting other civil and criminal business, including Gardaí, solicitors and, possibly, barristers, it would be stretching the word 'informal' beyond recognition to describe the atmosphere in which the claim will be heard as informal.

"Intimidating" was how one claimant who experienced that scene in a non-urban court, described her experience. That, in a word, is one of the problems that has been highlighted by people who experienced the system in some centres outside the main urban areas. Where there is uniformity in courtrooms being used exclusively for the hearing of small claims, rather than small claims being included in a very mixed list of cases, this problem will have dissipated.

PREPARATION

The preparation for a hearing is essential, whether one comes to the court as a claimant or as a respondent. This is as true for a small claims case in the District Court as it is for a multi-million Euro claim in the High Court, albeit the small claims procedure is designed so that solicitors and barristers are not needed.

However, if a claimant chooses to engage a solicitor to represent them, and even if they win the case and are awarded the maximum amount of €1,269.74 that the court is empowered to award, they will not be awarded costs. People who bring claims are responsible for paying their own costs. The whole point of the small claims procedure is that a person can bring a claim without using a solicitor. Therefore, if legal fess are incurred, they cannot be added to the amount of the claim, no matter how meritorious the claim and how despicable the behaviour or attitude of the respondent.

The same rule applies to a respondent. In preparing to defend a claim and, possibly, mounting a counterclaim against the claimant in the process, a respondent cannot expect to be awarded his legal costs if he succeeds in his defence and counterclaim, if there is one. If fees are incurred, the party employing the lawyer(s) must discharge them from their own resources.

Some corporate respondents employ solicitors on a regular basis to defend small claims brought against them. They do this as a matter of policy. These claims might be worth no more than a few hundred Euro in value but yet they are stoutly defended by lawyers whose fees will be paid by their client. While there is no suggestion that there is anything improper about this, critics could argue that it flies in the face of what the small claims procedure is meant to be – a service designed to handle small claims cheaply without involving a solicitor and in which the judge will conduct the hearing in an informal manner so as to do substantial justice between the parties.

WITNESSES

A question claimants and respondents frequently ask when preparing their case for court is whether they can call a witness. The answer is that of course they can. The evidence of a witness can be fundamental to success or failure for any litigant. However, if a party incurs expense in bringing somebody to the court, or to a hearing with the Registrar for that matter, they remain responsible for that expense.

Sometimes, the evidence of an expert witness, such as an engineer, is necessary to prove the actual basis of a claim or, on the other hand, to try on behalf of a respondent to controvert evidence given on behalf of a claimant. This type of evidence can be absolutely crucial to either party in any case where such expert evidence is required. But, no matter how crucial or important the expert evidence might be, the court has no discretion to award the successful party the cost of bringing that witness to court. The judge's hands are tied. Reports prepared by experts and witnesses' expenses must be paid by the party relying on them.

If possible, a claimant should try and get the witness to attend voluntarily. A frequently asked question is what can be done, if anything, if a witness refuses to attend. Is there anything the claimant can do to force a reluctant witness to attend and give evidence? If requested, the Small Claims Registrar will issue a witness summons on behalf of the party to "subpoena" the attendance of the witness at the court hearing. The fee for this service is €9. The requesting party, provided he or she is over the age of 18 years, could also personally serve the summons on the witness.

The issuing of witness summonses for claimants is extremely rare because most witnesses attend voluntarily and do not need to be coerced into attending court.

Respondents are more likely to bring witnesses to support the defence.

GUIDELINES

The following are some guidelines to consider which will assist a party pursuing a claim, whether the person is a claimant seeking money for damaged goods, a respondent seeking money in a counterclaim, or a respondent claiming that he owes the claimant nothing.

* Mark the court date on a calendar which is often looked at. Be in court on the day appointed for the hearing. If the date is missed, the case may be dismissed.

* It is essential to allow plenty of time to get to the court, so that when the party arrives they should be prepared to have their case heard immediately. They should therefore arrive at the court in as relaxed a state as possible and should not appear rushed and flustered. Otherwise, they will find it difficult to come to terms with the atmosphere of the court and send the wrong signals to the opposing party who may have arrived in good time and will, consequently, appear in a relaxed state of mind.

* Have everything that is needed to present the case properly. This may include such items as books, papers, documents, receipts, cancelled checks and photographs. These should be put in the order in which they are needed for presentation to the judge. What is needed in any particular case will depend on the type of claim being taken. However, the best advice is to bring anything you think will help to prove the claim to the judge.

* Make sure all the witnesses, if any, necessary to prove your case, are present in the courtroom

* Be prepared to give details of the claim to the judge when asked for them. This should be prepared for by making notes to yourself or otherwise in the period leading up to the hearing. In this respect, practice your

presentation to the court before the appointed day. Many others, including solicitors and barristers, do it, so do not be shy or feel awkward about it. The more familiar a person is with the case they want to present, the less self-conscious they will be in the witness box.

- Remember, even the most difficult of cases are capable of being settled. All things considered, a belief that one's case is incapable of settlement or compromise is erroneous. The most serious of cases with a value of millions of Pounds or Euros have settled in the High Court. Be prepared to settle at all times, before, during or even after the case has opened in court. If the claim is settled, the terms of settlement should be written down and given to the Registrar as soon as possible. This is imperative in case the other party refuses to comply, and refuses to pay in which case the party relying on the settlement terms may enforce the terms, in the manner indicated in the previous chapter.

- Since it is not unusual for problems to arise which makes it impossible or imprudent to go ahead with the hearing on the appointed day, either party can apply to the judge to adjourn the case to a later date. They will have to convince the judge that the reason is genuine. The better the reason a party to a claim has for not being ready to go on, the more likely the judge will be swayed into granting the application. It is very advisable to notify the opposing party in advance that an adjournment application will be made.

WHEN THE CASE IS CALLED

It is the most natural thing in the world for a claimant to experience feelings of extreme nervousness in advance of the case being called. In fact, it can be so extreme for some people that they do not hear their case being called and they only become aware of it when it is repeated or when somebody nearby draws their attention to it with words such as: "Is that your case?" When it does sink in, however, the butterflies can have a field day, but it is surprising that once they begin to answer questions, they 'find their feet' and confidence returns.

When the case is called, the claimant should walk forward to the front of the court. The case will be conducted by the judge in an informal way. He or she will do everything to put the parties at their ease and will understand the emotions that people not familiar to appearing in court will have and make allowances for it.

THE EVIDENCE

The judge may already have a good idea of what the case is about. The file from the District Court office will be available to the court, including the particulars of claim and the respondent's notice of dispute with his reasons for defending the claim. Whether the judge has prior knowledge, the claimant will be called to the witness box to give evidence of the claim after taking the oath, or affirmation, to tell the truth, the whole truth and nothing but the truth.

The claimant will detail the most important features of the claim, and with promptings from the judge, will give answers to specific questions from the bench (the judge). During that period, any documentary evidence that the claimant has to support the case will be presented to the judge. When the claimant has concluded giving direct evidence or evidence-in-chief, as it is sometimes referred to, the respondent (or perhaps a solicitor representing the respondent) will stand up and direct a number of questions to the claimant. This is cross-examination. When that stage has ended, the judge may ask one or two questions of the claimant, in order to tease out the issues or get a better understanding of them. The claimant may then call a witness to support the claim being made. Again, the witness will give direct evidence before being cross-examined on that evidence by the respondent. In most cases, that represents the totality of the evidence for the claimant.

It then becomes the turn of the respondent to make his case. It follows the exact same pattern as that of the claimant. The respondent or a representative of the respondent gives evidence and is cross-examined by the claimant before any supporting witness or witnesses are called to give their evidence. Again, they are liable to be questioned by the claimant in the form of cross-examination. The claimant should:

- Remember that they have the burden of proving their side of the story on the balance of probabilities.
- Not argue with the judge.
- Be courteous to the judge and to the opposing party.
- Not interrupt the judge or any other person when they are speaking.
- Have the documentary evidence available to the judge.

THE JUDGMENT

When all the evidence has concluded, the judge will invariably give reasons for coming to the conclusion he or she has arrived at and then will enter judgment for either the claimant or the respondent. There is no hard and fast rule as to how any particular case will conclude. Each case is judged on its own merits. If the judge finds that the respondent is liable to the claimant, it means that the claimant has succeeded in getting over the major hurdle, the issue of liability. The judge will then go on to decide the amount of Euros that the claimant is entitled to. This will have been adverted to during the claimant's evidence because it is for the claimant to prove the amount of the claim. Depending on the circumstances of each case, all that may be required to prove this aspect of the claim is the production to the court of a receipt for the original product, for instance.

What happens next depends on the outcome of the particular case:

- If the claim is resolved to the satisfaction of the claimant, the respondent will be formally notified of the court's decision a few days after the hearing. The notification will also inform the respondent that he will be allowed four (4) weeks in which to pay the amount decreed by the court.
- If the claimant is unsuccessful, the judge will dismiss the case.
- If the respondent is successful in bringing a counterclaim against the claimant, the claimant will be ordered to pay the amount of money decided by the judge.
- It is open to either party to bring an appeal against the decision of the judge to the Circuit Court.
- Such appeals are uncommon, indeed rare, for one very practical reason, cost. The parties will normally be represented by solicitor and barristers in the Circuit Court. Unlike the Small Claims Court, the court will grant the successful party their costs of the appeal and since the amount of those costs will be very much larger than the maximum amount of the decree, €1,269.74, that the court is empowered to award, it would be foolish in the extreme for an unsuccessful claimant to take such an appeal. The same financial considerations may not apply to a corporate respondent which may feel compelled to bring an appeal on an important point of principle such as that the Small Claims Court decision may have been an important test case for other similar claims waiting in the wings for the outcome.

In the next two chapters we will examine ways in which a successful party enforces a decree of the Small Claims Court.

CHAPTER 7

THE SHERIFF

Mention the name of the sheriff and thoughts evoke of the American *Wild West*, cowboys and Indians. Mention the bailiff and thoughts return to nearer home and scenes of destitution, especially during the dark days of Irish history. The reality is that neither has gone away. The sheriff and the bailiff have not disappeared into the dim and distant past but are very much part of everyday life in this country. They play a crucial role in the Small Claims Procedure.

When the District Court judge gives judgment and holds in favour of a claimant, the court does not pay out the amount that is awarded; it just rules on which party is liable to pay and quantifies the amount due. While the findings can be appealed at that point to the Circuit Court, assuming that there are good grounds to do so, a party should never file an appeal purely on the ground that they disagree with the judge's ruling. Strictly speaking, professional advice should be sought to establish if grounds of appeal exist at all. If an appeal is to be taken, contact should be made with the court offices as soon as possible as there is a strict time limit, which must be adhered to. The particular rule (Order 101) of the District Court covering this situation states:

> "Every appeal from a decision of a Justice to a Judge of the Circuit Court shall be by notice signed by the party appealing or his solicitor. The notice of appeal shall be lodged with the Clerk of the Court Area in which the decision appealed from shall have been given within **seven days** from the date on which such decision shall have been given and such notice shall also be served on the opposing party within the said period of seven days.

The notice of appeal shall be made to the appropriate Circuit Court to be held next after the said period of seven days."

As stated, appeals from the small Claims Court are only taken in the rarest circumstances, and then only by unsuccessful respondents or more correctly unsuccessful corporate respondents because the costs of legal representation by solicitor and barrister will be ordered against the unsuccessful party.

However, reverting back to the Small Claims Court, if the claim is decided in favour of the claimant, the respondent will be notified of the court's decision a few days after the hearing and will be allowed a generous period of about four weeks to pay the amount awarded by the court. Something that people should remember is that those who are successful in their claims are responsible for collecting the money. However, there is one avenue that can be pursued with the assistance of the Small Claims Registrar immediately it becomes apparent that the respondent is not lodging an appeal and is not paying the decree. It is by way of execution, the legal process of enforcing a judgment. Enter the local Sheriff. Dublin City, Cork City and Dublin County have individual sheriffs, while the functions of the Sheriff are performed in counties throughout the country by the County Registrar for each county.

IF THE RESPONDENT FAILS TO PAY UP

If the respondent does not pay, the claimant can apply to the Small Claims Registrar to have the order of the court sent to the Sheriff to get the money or, for execution, to use the appropriate term. For this service, the claimant has to pay €7.62 in respect of the Sheriff's fee. This money will be refunded to the claimant if the Sheriff is successful in executing the court order.

A reasonable question to ask is how does the Sheriff operate where the collection or execution of small claims decrees are concerned. While one would expect that these are easily enforced because only reasonably small amounts of money are involved, in fact the opposite is the case. These are the most difficult of all to collect.

When the process is started, the Sheriff's office is issued with a decree by the Small Claims Registrar (see sample Small Claims Decree (Summary Judgment) form at **Appendix B**). It is signed by both the judge of the District Court and the Small Claims Registrar and it is then up to the Sheriff or County Registrar, as the case may be, to put the procedure known as *fieri facias* into effect. This is often referred to as a *fi fa*. It is a very old procedure or method under which the Sheriff can seize the goods and chattels of the debtor and have them sold. The proceeds of the sale will be used to pay the claimant the amount owed under the decree, less the expenses of the execution, which is 3.5% of the debt. The claimant will be refunded the €7.62 fee paid in respect of the Sheriff's fee.

NO GOODS

Sometimes disputes arise with regard to which goods can be seized by the Sheriff. However, there is a procedure available which can resolve such disputes In any event, the sheriff or county registrar, as the case may be, will eventually make a return to the Small Claims Registrar in which the results of the attempts at execution are revealed. If they have failed to take any goods, the return will state *nulla bona*. This means no goods were taken and is bad news for the claimant who is waiting in the wings for his or her money.

This can arise in different situations, including where the debtor has only leased goods in his possession or where the available goods are jointly owned with another person. It might also be the case that the only goods are fixtures such as dry cleaning dryers and other plant in the case of a dry cleaner. In this situation it would not be practicable for the Sheriff or the County Registrar to remove them and then to try and sell them, especially in the case of a decree of €200 or €300 from the Small Claims Court in respect of a cardigan damaged in the dry cleaners. It would just not be worth the time, difficulty and expense of removing the plant and machinery to meet such a small debt.

On the other hand, if the Sheriff or County Registrar is successful, they will arrange for the sale of the seized goods for the best price available in the particular circumstances.

Small claims debtors or respondents have to be pursued quite vigorously, according to one Sheriff. They are often the most difficult to collect from. As advised earlier in this book, it is absolutely essential that the claimant should make certain of the exact respondent in any given case. The Sheriff's experience is that the judgment is given against the wrong party in many instances. That is not the fault of the court but of the claimant who did not make a proper search to establish the true identity of the respondent before filling in the details of the respondent in the forms, the application to the Registrar and in the notice of claim against the respondent.

Sometimes, a respondent is named in the decree as an individual or a name under which the business traded whereas the respondent should be the company that owned the business. Similarly, where homebuilders are concerned, the proper respondent might be an individual instead of a company. If the wrong party is named as respondent, it ties the hands of the sheriff or county registrar.

THE PRACTICE

In practice, in the experience of the Sheriff we spoke to, the collection rate of small claims decrees is good.

Briefly, when the Sheriff first receives the decree from the court, a letter is sent to the respondent debtor directing him to pay the amount of the decree but warning him that his goods would be seized unless payment is received. If that letter is ignored, a bailiff goes out to visit the respondent and shows the decree personally to the respondent. This is a "face to face" confrontation, and he warns the respondent to pay the amount due. If the respondent still ignores this demand, it is obvious that mere threats are having no effect. The matter is then referred to the Sheriff's seizure department and in those circumstances, the bailiff assembles a team of helpers and travel by truck to the respondent's address to execute the warrant.

If the goods are seized, everybody gets paid. In practice, in the experience of the Sheriff for County Dublin, the collection rate is good. Just how good is apparent from the following results for the year ended December 31, 2002:

The Sheriff was sent a total of 74 small claims decrees by the Small Claims Registrars in the various District Courts in Co. Dublin. Of that number, the Sheriff succeeded in getting the respondents to pay in 43 of those cases. Of the balance, 27 were returned as 'no goods' or else the respondent had left the address given for them in the court documents, while only four were still being dealt with four months later. These results would be the average for each year.

COUNTY WICKLOW

A total of 18 decrees were sent to the County Registrar in the case of the Small Claims Courts in Co. Wicklow from the main office in Bray. Of these, 12 were enforced and only one was returned marked 'no goods.'

If these are representative samples of how the Sheriffs and County Registrars fare in their efforts to enforce small claims decrees, it speaks volumes for the system of enforcement relied on by the Small Claims Courts. However, in chapter 8 we will look at other methods of enforcement.

CHASING THE DEBTOR BY OTHER MEANS

It is all very well for a person to go through the preparation, worry and even trauma of taking a claim through the Small Claims Procedure and to win. But what if the respondent does not forward a cheque for the amount of the decree awarded by the court to the claimant. The judgment of the court is useless if it cannot be enforced.

Any person who succeeds in getting a decree for a sum of money from the Small Claims Court should be able to avail of whatever machinery is available with the rules of court to enforce that order against the other party. Otherwise, the losing party could whistle a tune and walk away from his or her obligations without a care in the world. If they have been found by a court to be in default and, short of bringing an appeal to the Circuit Court which they have every right to do, they must pay up. That is the reality of being held liable by the court.

In Chapter 7 we have seen the process by which unpaid decrees are sought to be executed by the Sheriff. In some instances, the Sheriff's efforts are fruitless and the successful claimant is left without his decree. There are a number of other avenues available to him that could be explored.

INSTALMENT ORDER

A good device often lost sight of for getting a debtor to meet his obligations to the creditor and to the court is a process under which a creditor will apply to the District Court for an order directing the debtor to pay the sum due by instalment. However, the debtor will first be brought before the court and be examined as to his means.

The 1977 District Court Rules make provision for this method, which creditors can use to bring pressure to bear on parties who refuse are unwilling to pay the amount of the decree. The respondent in the case before the Small Claims Court, is known in the rules governing the procedure detailed below as a debtor while the successful party, the claimant, for example, becomes known as the creditor. Of course, if the claimant was successfully sued for a decree in the Small Claims Court on a counterclaim by the respondent and refused to pay it or did not pay it, they would then become known as the debtor.

Rule 3(1) of Order 53 of the District Court Rules which deals with the enforcement of judgments, provides that whenever a debt is due on foot of a judgment of a competent court (which the Small Claims Court is) and the creditor wishes to enforce that judgment, the creditor or his solicitor, can arrange for the attendance of the debtor in court for an examination of the debtor's means by the judge. They do this by lodging a summons in duplicate with the Clerk of the District Court. This procedure has formed part of the District Court Rules for many years. It dates back to 1926 when the Enforcement of Court Orders Act was enacted and it was amended by section 1(1) of the Courts (No.2) Act 1986.

The Clerk will list the matter for hearing after completing and signing the original and a copy of the summons that are then issued to the creditor or his or her solicitor who will have them served on the debtor.

No person or party would look forward or would submit lightly to having their financial affairs scrutinised by a judge in open court. But that is the prospect facing such a defaulter if they fail to discharge the debt.

EXAMINATION UNDER OATH

For the purpose of the examination of the debtor by the judge, the debtor has first to lodge a document known as a statement of means with the court and this must be done not less than one week before the date fixed for the hearing of the examination. The creditor or his solicitor is entitled to go into the court's office and inspect the debtor's statement of means. They can also take copies of it any time after it is lodged.

The statement of means must set out the debtor's assets and liabilities, his total income and the means by which it is earned together with the sources of that income. It must also include the names of those people to whom he is legally or morally responsible for their support.

At the actual examination hearing, the creditor or his solicitor must produce the judgment of the court, in this case the Small Claims Court, on which reliance is placed, a certificate (Form 53.4 Schedule C in the appendix to the Rules) signed by the creditor or his solicitor showing how much of the debt remained outstanding at the date of the certificate. A copy of the certificate must have been furnished to the debtor or his solicitor prior to the date of the examination hearing.

The debtor has to swear the oath or other affirmation so that he is bound to answer the judge's questions truthfully. The debtor can produce evidence as to his means. The creditor may also produce evidence of the debtor's means. Child benefit, other social welfare payments and allowances as well as widows' pensions and other pensions would not be taken into account by the judge when assessing the debtor's means. If the judge concludes that the statement of means filed by the debtor is materially inaccurate to the debtor's knowledge, the debtor can be sent to prison.

If, having heard all of the evidence, the judge is satisfied that the debtor has the means to discharge the debt, either in one sum or by way of instalments, he can make an order directing the debtor to pay the amount of the decree in the case of the Small Claims Court. The judge can, and usually does, make an order for the costs of the examination process to be paid by the debtor.

An instalment order could, for example, order a debtor to pay the amount of the decree of say €1,000 by weekly payments of €20. It is worth noting that after the District Court judge makes an instalment order, either the debtor or the creditor can serve a summons on the other party in which a variation of the instalment order was being sought. This, of course, would necessitate both parties returning to the District Court. One way in which this could happen would be where the creditor became aware of the fact that the debtor had 'come into money' such as by an increase in salary or by other means.

Unless the debt and costs have been paid in full, an instalment order remains in force for 12 years from the date of the judgment to which it relates.

PRISON

In this country a person cannot be sent to prison for not paying his debts. The Debtors (Ireland) Act 1872 prohibited imprisonment for non-payment of debts. However, a person can be imprisoned for failing to obey a court order. Failing to abide by an order of a court is contempt of court and is punishably by several means, including imprisonment. It depends on what view the judge takes of the breach of the order. Therefore, any person who is subject to an instalment order and breaches that order by refusing or failing to pay the sums fixed by the court as they fall due risks being sent to prison. The period in prison cannot be longer than 12 weeks.

People who find themselves in that situation should know that the fact that imprisonment is imposed does not discharge the debt.

It is relevant to ask what issues will weigh on the mind of the judge when deciding whether to send the debtor to prison. Before sending a person in these circumstances to prison, the judge must be satisfied that the failure by the debtor to pay was due either to his wilful refusal or to his culpable neglect. As we have seen, the law was changed in 1872. As a result we can say with some certainty that a person's inability to pay such a debt will never result in a prison term being imposed. The judge will only impose a prison sentence where he thinks it is proper in the circumstances. In other words, the judge has absolute discretion when to impose a prison sentence. As we said earlier, each case is judged on its own circumstances and that is as true of the judge sitting adjudicating a claim in the Small Claims Court as it is of a judge deciding whether to send a person to prison for breach of an instalment order

If the money, the subject matter of the debt, is paid to the clerk of the court or to the prison governor before the prison sentence is served, the person must be released from custody immediately. The Minister for Justice may also intervene in these type of situations and order the release from prison of the debtor either unconditionally or on condition that all or portion of the outstanding debt be discharged.

OTHER METHODS OF ENFORCING PAYMENT

There are other methods of enforcing judgments in an effort to secure payment but, in all honesty, given the small sums involved in the small claims procedure – less than €1,300 – it would be too expensive and too cumbersome to put in place to make the exercise worthwhile.

These would include charging orders and attachment of stocks and shares where, for example, the shares of a private company, which owned the business found liable to the claimant by the court, could be charged for the amount of the decree.

These methods of enforcement would also include a system known as garnishee. A garnishee is a third party who owes money to the debtor or, more correctly, the judgment debtor. When the creditor finds out that money is due to the debtor from a third party, the garnishee, the creditor can apply to the court for an order to attach that money and have it paid to discharge the debt to him. The money must be paid to him by the garnishee and to nobody else. Before a court will order the attachment, there must be a court judgment. A decree of the Small Claims Court would certainly qualify.

One of the benefits of using this procedure to enforce the court's decree is that the debtor will not want it to be known by his other creditors that there is a court judgment against him. Notice of intention by the creditor to seek the garnishee.

DETERRENT

Of all these, the very threat of having to undergo such a public examination of one's means, let alone the spectre of a period in prison, may well be enough to secure immediate payment of a decree.

CHAPTER 9

AN EU INITIATIVE
FOR SMALL CLAIMS

The publication of this book is coinciding with an initiative from the Commission of European Union that may lead to the introduction in Member States of a European order for payment procedure and measures to simplify and speed up small claims litigation. Earlier this year, a Green Paper was issued by the Commission, which was designed to encourage a wide-ranging consultation of possible measures to be taken at Community level.

The Green Paper deals with proposals in two distinct areas of procedural laws: a specific procedure for the speedy and efficient recovery of uncontested claims which would be a European order for payment procedure and, secondly, a proposal for the simplification and acceleration of small claims. This chapter is concerned with the latter. These proposed European instruments will be the first initiatives in the field of civil and judicial co-operation directly concerning the rules that govern the procedure to obtain an enforceable decision.

Before looking at how the Green Paper deals with the small claims issue specifically, the paper invites comment on two questions it addresses concerning both procedures: Should European instruments on order for payment proceedings and on small claims be applicable to cross-border cases only or to purely internal litigation? Secondly, it asks for comment on whether the proposed legislative instrument in both cases should be in the form of a regulation or a directive.

With regard to the small claims proposal, the Paper notes that there seems to be a growing concern among EU citizens and by small and medium-seized enterprises in the Community that their judicial systems do not fully meet their demands.

> "For many the judicial system is too expensive, too slow and too difficult to deal with. The smaller the claim is, the more the weight of these obstacles increases, since costs, delay and vexation do not necessarily decrease proportionally with the amount of the claim. These problems have led to the creation of simplified civil procedures for *Small Claims* in many Member States."

At the same time, the potential number of cross-border disputes is rising as a consequence of the increasing use of the EC Treaty rights of free movement of persons, goods and services. The obstacles to getting a fast and inexpensive judgment are intensified in a cross-border context: it would be necessary to hire two lawyers and there were translation and interpretation costs and travel costs for lawyers, litigants and witnesses. In addition, there is a wide range of other issues, including the following:

- Individuals may be involved in an accident while on holiday or while making a shopping trip abroad, or

- They may buy goods which later turn out to be faulty or dangerous.

- A consumer may use the Internet to order goods from abroad which are never dispatched or which turn out to be faulty.

- A hotel owner should be able to pursue a customer who left without paying his bill. The expense of obtaining a judgment against a defendant in another Member State is often disproportionate to the amount of money involved. Many people, faced with the expense of the proceedings, and daunted by the practical difficulties that are likely to ensue, abandon any hope of obtaining what they believe is rightfully theirs.

"The European Union faces the challenge of ensuring that in a genuine European Area of Justice individuals and businesses are not prevented or discouraged from exercising their rights by the incompatibility or complexity of the legal and judicial systems in the Member States. Since this problem is particularly virulent in the case of *Small Claims*, action has been considered most urgent in this specific field of civil procedure" said the consultation document.

This is the third time, at least, in which the issue of small claims has been tackled at Community level. In a 1996 action plan, the Commission proposed the introduction of a simplified European form in order to improve the access to court procedures while in 1998, it proposed the introduction of small claims procedures in all Member States.

EXISTING SMALL CLAIMS PROCEDURES IN MEMBER STATES

In the lead up to the publication of the Green Paper, the Commission distributed a questionnaire to all the Member States to get a description of national procedures. There was no answer from Greece but, in fact, that country does have a Small Claims Procedure. In Italy, there is a specific procedure which is not simplified procedurally. Instead, the judge decides on claims below €1,000 not on the basis of law, but of equity (fairness).

Simplified procedures for small claims exist not only in Ireland but also in Germany, Spain, France, Sweden and the United Kingdom. Their most important characteristics are:

- In Ireland, Spain, Sweden and the UK (England/Wales, Scotland and Northern Ireland) there are specific Small Claims Procedures, which provide for various simplifications with respect to the ordinary procedure. In many cases, the introduction of the claim is facilitated, often through a specific form. Certain rules concerning the taking of evidence are relaxed, and the possibility of purely written procedure exists. Also, the possibility of to appeal is excluded or restricted.

- In Germany, there is no specific procedure for small claims, but courts may determine their procedures as they see fit in small claims cases.

- In France, there is no specific procedure for small claims, but there is a simplified way of introducing the procedure at the Tribunal by a simple declaration

- There are no specific procedures for small claims in Austria, Belgium, Denmark, Finland, Luxembourg, the Netherlands and Portugal.

MONETARY LIMITS IN EACH STATE

Some of the most important features of the existing Small Claims Procedures are summarised as follows:

There is considerable variation in the monetary thresholds for these procedures. In Germany it is €600, in Scotland it is €1,235 in small claims intended to be used by the lay person and €2,470 in consumer claim actions by corporate bodies for recovery of debt and claims by landlords to recover possession of heritable property; €1,269.74 (this was erroneously stated as €1,270 in the Green Paper); €2,038 in Sweden; €3,005 in Spain; €3,294 (Northern Ireland); €3,811 in France; and €8,234 in England/Wales).

In Germany, England/Wales, Scotland, Spain and Sweden the use of the simplified procedure is obligatory for claims below the threshold of the particular State, but in most of those Member States a litigation can be transferred to the ordinary or a more formal procedure by the judge or on application of a party. In Ireland and France the small claims procedure is optional. In Northern Ireland, claims for less than Sterling £2,000 are subject to the small claims procedure, unless the proceedings are for a debt or liquidated amount and the claimant opts to proceed by ordinary civil bill. However, even then the defendant may serve a notice of intention to defend that is endorsed with a request that the matter be dealt with as a small claim and the court is obliged to acceded to that request.

INTRODUCTION OF THE PROCEDURE

Forms can be used for filing the claim in Ireland, England/Wales, Scotland, Northern Ireland, Sweden, Spain and France. There is no form filling in Germany but all applications and declarations can also be made orally. In Austria, the claim can be entered in the record of the District Court at the place of residence of the claimant which will establish the competent court and transfer the case to it.

NO OBLIGATION TO ENGAGE A LAWYER

There is no obligation to make legal references in the application in any Member State. In other words, the court in each State is concerned only with facts. "Accordingly, claimants do not necessarily have to employ a lawyer."

ASSISTANCE

In most States, (Ireland, Germany, England/Wales, Scotland, Northern Ireland, Sweden and Austria), support is given by a court clerk or help desk for the introduction of a procedure. Also, the judges give assistance during the hearing to a party not represented by a lawyer, particularly on procedural issues, while observing the principle of impartiality (Ireland, Sweden, France, Germany, England/Wales, Northern Ireland and Austria.)

At present, no Member State requires mandatory representation by a lawyer in small claims procedures. In France, the parties in practice often defend themselves without assistance by a lawyer and come to the hearing with a more or less complete file.

ALTERNATIVE DISPUTE RESOLUTION

In several Member States, Alternative Dispute Settlement methods have been introduced in the context of court proceedings. In Ireland, the Green Paper notes, efforts are directly connected with the Small Claims Procedure. The Registrar facilitates conciliation, mediation and informal discussion in an effort to reach a settlement without a judgment being delivered.

Other Member States have provisions to facilitate ADR in the context of court proceedings, independently of existing (or not existing) Small Claims Procedures. These provisions range from granting the possibility of recourse to ADR (for example in Belgium and France) to its encouragement in Spain, Italy, Sweden and England/Wales, and even the prior obligation to have recourse to ADR under the law or by decision of the judge in Germany, Belgium and Greece.

RELAXING THE RULES OF EVIDENCE

In Small Claims Procedures in England/Wales and Northern Ireland the strict rules of evidence do not apply. In England/Wales no expert may give evidence, whether written or oral, at a hearing without the permission of the court.

In Scotland and Sweden, the normal rules of evidence are relaxed. In Scotland, there is a hearing with a further hearing for evidence when necessary. Written statements of witnesses are regarded as documentary evidence. In Germany, the courts are free to obtain evidence as they see fit and are not bound by statutory rules of evidence or evidential procedures. The discretion of the court is limited however by the principle of a fair hearing, the right to a hearing in law, the prohibition of arbitrariness and the principle of reasonability and of impartiality.

The courts in Austria can reject the taking of evidence proposed by the parties in cases with claims below €1,000.

In England and Wales, Northern Ireland, Sweden and Germany, telephone conferences are possible.

In Ireland, Spain, Sweden and Germany witnesses can submit written statements instead of appearing before the court. In Northern Ireland, written statements of witnesses are possible but not widely used.

COSTS

In many Member States all the costs have to be paid by the defendant alone if he loses. In Ireland, England/Wales, Scotland, France, Sweden and Northern Ireland, the reimbursement of costs is limited. It varies from no reimbursement in Ireland to restrictions on court fees in Northern Ireland and fixed maximum sums, in some cases depending on the value of the claim, in England/Wales, Scotland and Sweden).

APPEALS

In Ireland and Spain it is possible to appeal against the judgment of the small claims court without limitation. In Scotland, an appeal is only possible on a point of law. In Sweden, an appeal is subject to permission that is granted if there are particular circumstances such as the importance of the case for the application of the law. In England/Wales, an appeal is subject to permission in all cases except for specific instances that effect the liberty of the individual.

In Northern Ireland there is a very restricted right of appeal in small claims proceedings. The District Court judge may, and must if ordered by the High Court to do so, state for the determination of the High Court any question of law arising out of an award.

In France the threshold for taking an appeal is €3,811 and in Germany it is €600 which effectively mean that in a small claims procedure an appeal is not possible. In Germany, an appeal is nevertheless admitted if the case is of general significance. In Austria, an appeal against judgments concerning claims below €2,000 is possible only because of nullity (i.e. most severe procedural errors) or on points of law. Appeals based on factual points and evaluation of evidence are excluded.

QUESTIONS

The Green Paper posed a considerable number of questions related to the material produced above but since the responses had to be submitted to the European Commission by May 31, 2003; there was little to achieve in reproducing them in this publication. If a second edition of this book becomes a reality, the matter will be looked at again. In the meantime, the information gleaned from the Green Paper gives a valuable insight into the operation of the small claims procedure on a very broad front indeed.

CHAPTER 10

CASE HISTORIES

The Small Claims Court is asked to adjudicate on cases, which are extremely varied in their type and monetary value. On any given day that the District Court sits exclusively to hear small claims –this happens in Dublin and Cork - there might be as many as ten cases listed, although some may be applications to set aside decrees already granted against respondents who failed to respond to, or defend, a claim.

While the maximum amount of money that the court can award is 26 cents less than €1,270, the amount being claimed can be extremely small. There is no lower limit to the amount of money a person may claim. One case serves to illustrate this.

CASE AGAINST JEWELLERY SHOP

After taking the oath to tell the truth, the whole truth and nothing but the truth, a woman told the Small Claims Court that she walked into a Dublin jewellery shop with a piece of antique jewellery that could be used on a chain or necklace. Two stones on the piece were loose and she wanted advice as to what it would cost to repair. She specifically told the two shop assistants who attended her that she did not want the jewellery repaired. The jewellery had to be outsourced to another jeweller and she was told it would take three weeks. "I was extremely specific that I only wanted advice," the woman testified.

When she returned to the shop to collect her jewellery and to receive the advice she had sought, she found out that the jewellery had been repaired, contrary to her instructions. Not alone that but she was dissatisfied with the repair work that had, in fact, been carried out. In order to get her jewellery back she had to pay €65 and she was now claiming that amount of money from the jewellery shop.

There are small claims and there are small claims, but this case certainly fitted into the smallest category of cases that come before the court. It would generally be expected that such a small claim would never see the light of day, that the parties would reach a settlement or compromise long before it would be listed for hearing but as is so often the case, people adopt attitudes and become reluctant, indeed steadfast, to move from their stated position, despite the best efforts of the Registrar to negotiate a settlement.

When the claimant had concluded giving her direct evidence, the jeweller who was the principal of the business the claimant was suing, got his chance to cross-examine her. Very often at this stage the respondent will start to outline his own position, by giving direct evidence but the judge will quickly remind them that their turn will come to go into the witness box to give their direct evidence under oath.

Replying to him, the claimant said she had told the two assistants in his shop that she was worried the "fine bezel" would be removed from the jewellery if the two stones were removed from it. She was concerned that the two assistants were not writing down her instructions and she repeated that she only wanted advice and did not want it repaired. That concluded the evidence for the claimant who did not call any witness to give evidence on her behalf.

Asked for his response to the evidence of the claimant that she had given instructions that no repairs were to be done, the respondent, after being sworn, said they had sent the piece of jewellery to an expert.

Judge: She didn't want it repaired.

Respondent: He (expert) told me what was required and that it would be reasonable. I told him to go ahead.

Answering the claimant, he said he thought the charges for

the repair were reasonable. Anybody who was trying to get something repaired would be satisfied.

Decision: Giving his decision the judge said: "She did not want any repairs carried out; she only wanted advice about two loose stones. She did not get advice; she got repairs and had to pay €65. I will give her a decree for €65."

RENT DEPOSIT CASE

As many people know when renting a house, a flat or apartment, it can often be difficult to secure a return of the deposit which might amount to a full month's rent, Many cases which come before the Small Claims Court are concerned with the non-return of rent deposits or security deposits, as they are sometimes called, or even key money, by landlords who hold onto the deposit after expiry of the lease for any number of reasons, but most likely for damage caused by the tenants or lessees to the property, furniture or fittings. Such claims by landlords are invariably disputed by tenants and lessees who feel that landlords will use any excuse to hold onto the money.

Sometimes, the lessees or tenants never get to meet the landlord. In fact, they might not even know his, her or its name because they may, for instance, have dealt with an agent of the landlord.

One case such that came before the Small Claims Court was brought by a young woman who was claiming €854 security deposit on her own behalf and on behalf of a number of co-lessees of a house. The landlord held onto this money in respect of alleged damage to a table, for dry cleaning of curtains and outstanding refuse charges due to Dun Laoghaire Rathdown County Council. All of these were hotly disputed by the claimant who told the court that the house had been inspected by a representative of the agent before they left and everything was fine according to her. The refuse charges were due by a previous tenant and not by the four girls who shared the house. She had never seen a copy of the lease.

A member of the firm sued as agents of the landlord was unable to produce a copy of the lease at the judge's request.

Questioned by the agent's representative, the claimant said she did not know who the landlord was; she had asked the agent for the name of the landlord but it had never been furnished. She had only ever received correspondence from the agents and she had never seen a lease. She agreed there had been an assignment of her interest by one of the other girls in the house and a letter to that effect had been signed by the claimant.

The agent's representative, said the landlord had inspected the property after the girls moved out and had decided to make the deductions. He contended that the agents should not have been sued by the claimant. They did not hold the deposits.

Claimant: "We cannot take a claim against the landlord because we don't know who she is. You (agent's representative) said to take a claim against.........(she named the firm of agents they had dealt with and sued)."

Respondent: "We are agents for the landlords. She (landlord) should be standing here. We have no case to answer."

Judge: "You held yourselves out as her agents".

The agent's representative said he was a senior management agent for the couple who were the landlords. There was a lease agreement which had been drawn up by a solicitor, one counterpart was given to the lessees.

Of the money held back, €400 was in respect of French polishing of the dining room table, he said. He handed a docket to the judge which, said the judge, showed that €400 was in respect of French polishing not only the table but also a kitchen table and four chairs of which there had been no complaint. The agents were instructed by the landlords after the girls had left. Their (agent's) view was that the claim under the contract should be taken against the landlords, not against the agents.

Judge: "As far as I'm concerned this lady is entitled to get her money back. I saw no lease agreement. She did not know who the landlord was. I am satisfied you are agents and you are not entitled to deduct the money." He added that the landlord should have been in court to tell them what was wrong with the curtains and with the table which could not have become that "grubby" since the last inspection was carried out. In addition, the claimant said she had cleaned the cooker oven about which complaint had also been made by the landlord. The claimant was entitled to get her €854.92 back and he would grant a decree for that amount in her favour claimant against the respondent, the agents who, he advised, had a right to appeal his decision.

Decision: This decision was made in accordance with the civil law applicable in this country. The only way the respondent could legally question this decision was by taking an appeal to the Circuit Court. Such appeals are rarely taken. The question which arises is: should the agent have taken legal advice before deciding to defend the claim on the basis that he did? Taking professional advice would probably have saved him over €800, not to mention the time and aggravation involved in defending the claim. The agent should also have given consideration to having some form of protection under which his firm would be indemnified by the landlord of the property against such losses. However, questions of law are involved here and therefore would be a matter for the respondent and its legal adviser. Such decisions are useful pointers for the public and for business people generally. The regret is that so many important decisions made by the Small Claims Court are not reported in the popular media.

SECOND RENT DEPOSIT CASE

A young man who received a cheque for €300 in respect of his rent deposit from his landlady after he moved out of his shared apartment, only to have the cheque stopped by the landlady soon afterwards, was granted a decree for that amount by the Small Claims Court.

The claim arose out of a situation where, according to the young man, three others and himself paid a rent deposit total of €1,000 and when two of them moved out, they got their rent deposit back but he and another young man did not have theirs returned. He denied in the witness box that only three of them had moved in although the respondent landlady maintained that other young men were always coming and going. He informed the respondent that he was leaving and asked for his deposit to be paid into a bank account. A cheque for €300 was paid but it was subsequently cancelled. He had difficult in making contact with her after that. They had gone to Threshold to try and have the matter sorted out before going to court.

The respondent claimed they had damaged a door by playing darts but the claimant denied this saying they had no darts or a dartboard. He also denied that they had left the kitchen "in a state." The respondent had asked them to clean and polish the apartment before they left and they did that.

The respondent said the apartment was let to three people, not four and she received rent deposit of £750. There were only three beds in the apartment although they had brought in a couch themselves for their friend.

Judge: Why didn't you give him back £250 when he left?

Respondent: The place was left in a filthy mess. I filled a bin with the alcohol bottles they left behind. I asked him what happened to the door. I said 'Did you drive nails in it'? and he said 'no, it was must be darts'. She added that the claimant had telephoned her before he left the apartment saying he was desperate for the money and she gave him the cheque because she felt sorry for him. The claimant denied this.

Decision: The judge said he was satisfied that a total of £750 was paid to the respondent by three people. The respondent did not get any money from a fourth. The claimant was entitled to get the equivalent in Euros of £250 (€317.43) and he would give a decree for that amount. He advised the respondent to get a rent book and to have her property inspected before and after the tenants left. If there was something wrong, they should be informed in good time and not as in this case.

LOST BAGGAGE

Many of the claims made through the Small Claims Procedure relate to lost baggage by airlines. However, the policy of the judges in Small Claims Court is to award only the amount allowed by the Warsaw/Hague Convention which is about $20 per kilo, is small consolation for a person whose laptop computer goes missing with a month's work saved on its hard drive or for a passenger who purchased expensive clothing for a trip and carried it in a suitcase which failed to appear on the carousel in the baggage hall on arrival at a destination.

Travel insurance is an absolute must for all trips with airlines, whether it is a business trip or a holiday flight that is being undertaken.

Some airlines will negotiate with passengers with *bona fide* claims arising out of lost luggage, delayed flights and problems and very often arrive at a solution satisfactory from both perspectives. However, budget airlines will not, and customers are left with no option but to take a claim through small claims which are always vigorously defended by lawyers.

DEFECTIVE CAR

A sports car purchased in February 2002 from a garage for €7,000 without the buyer ever having driven it was found to have a knocking noise in the region of the left back wheel arch. In addition, the car did not handle properly. Subsequently, it was discovered on examination that the anti-roll bar had been dismantled, the front shocks were 'soft' and there was a hole in the exhaust pipe. All of this, despite the fact the car had passed its National Car Test six months earlier.

The owner of the garage where the car was bought said he had agreed to have the shocks changed and other repairs carried out but the claimant, a young man, said he preferred to have it done elsewhere because he did not get any satisfaction from the respondent when he brought the car back on a number of occasions. He had an estimate of €1,250 for parts, labour and VAT from another garage for the repairs to his car which was locked up in his garage at home.

Decision: Granting the claimant a decree for the total amount of €1,250, the judge said the car was obviously dangerous when the claimant purchased it. "I don't know how it passed its NCT in September, 2001," he added.

ANOTHER CLAIM AGAINST A GARAGE
Another young man who bought a car for €1,000 from a garage after being told by a man who claimed to be a mechanic that it had a good engine but which, it transpired, had numerous mechanical problems, including gearbox mounting, handbrake cable, side and hazard lights and brakeshoes, was granted a decree for €1,000 jointly against the garage where he purchased the car and the alleged mechanic who had advised him.

Claimant: The claimant said he learned subsequently that the man who advised man about the car was not a mechanic but was working in association with the garage owner. He sued both.

Judge: The judge advised the claimant: "When you buy a

car, have it examined by your own engineer. You trusted this man. I think you were duped."

There was no appearance in court by either of the respondents.

CHAPTER 11

STATISTICS

The Small Claims Procedure is more widely used in this country than is realised. The reason that the public are not aware of its success is because claims that qualify to be called small and tried as such by the District Court, are generally not reported in the media unless the details of the claim are unusual or unique.

Such a case made the headlines in some national broadsheet newspapers earlier this year when a woman brought an unsuccessful claim in the Dublin Small Claims Court against a cosmetic surgeon over a liposuction procedure carried out on her by the surgeon. Although she lost her claim, the court directed the surgeon to make an *ex-gratia* payment of €200 to the woman after he failed to respond to a letter of complaint from her. The woman sought the return of €1,000 of the €3,800 she paid for the procedure.

In 2001, the Small Claims Court granted a total of 444 decrees, a slight rise on the number granted the previous year, at 427. In all, the court dismissed 118 cases, compared with 98 in 2000. In addition, 317 cases were withdrawn or struck out in 2001 as against 318 the previous year. We will now consider the individual applications to see what category they fall into.

HOLIDAY CLAIMS

Claims arising out of holidays abroad are one of the most common forms of claim handled by the small claims system in this country. In both 2000 and 2001 they represented the single biggest category of applications received by the court. In 2001, the number of claims taken under this heading totalled 484. Large as that number was, it still represented a drop on the number of such claims taken the previous year when 530 applications were received.

As we saw in Chapter 8, this is one of the areas that the European Commission highlighted as for attention for the cross-border nature of the claim.

People going on holidays are familiar with the booking form they sign when paying their money. It will read something like: "I have read and understood the details provided in relation to the arbitration scheme, and agree that any dispute or difference of any kind which arises or occurs in relation to any thing or matter arising out of or in connection with this contract shall be referred to arbitration under the arbitration rules of the Chartered Institute of Arbitrators – Irish Branch. Alternatively, claims for less than the jurisdiction of the District Court Small Claims Procedure per booking form may be pursued through the small claims court." That means that claims up to a maximum of €1,269.74 arising out of holidays may be taken through the small claims procedure.

The obvious attraction of a holiday claim being taken in this way is that no costs will be incurred by either side. It can be disposed of quickly and cheaply, and while arbitration itself is regarded as being a cheaper form of dispute resolution than the ordinary courts, it is unquestionable that the small claims procedure outshines all other forums in many respects. Claims can relate to anything from a bad apartment or hotel experience to the taxi fares incurred as a result of delayed flights to or from a holiday destination.

RENT DEPOSITS

The next most popular form of claim is that taken by tenants against their landlords. What they seek is the rent deposit they paid when entering their lease, but which the landlord held onto for whatever reason when the lease or letting agreement came to an end. This is often referred to as key money, a term less known than rent deposit. In the year 2000, a total of 381 of these claims were received through the Small Claims Procedure nationally. However, the number of similar claims fell to 356 in 2001.

FURNITURE

Claims relating to furniture accounted for the third highest number of claims received in 2000 and 2001. In 2000, the number of furniture claims received was 256 but the number received the following year dropped to 218.

OTHER CLAIMS RECEIVED

Cars, electric goods, audio and computer equipment, damage to private property and professional services, dry cleaners, clothing and carpets were the subjects of many claims received in recent years. A total of 210 claims related to cars were taken in 2001, a jump from 180 received as small claims in the previous year. Claims in respect of electric goods were as popular as ever. In 2000, the number of such claims received was 228 but this number dropped to 207 in 2001.

Professional services accounted for 150 claims in 2001, a rise of 44 on the number of such claims received the previous year. Another hardy annual when it comes to claims are those arising out of small building works. There were 145 of these cases received in 2001, one more than in the previous year. As usual, there were some claims relating to the purchase of shoes. In 2001, there were 50 such claims received, a drop of 28 similar claims received in 2000. Carpets and flooring also accounted for a considerable number of claims. In 2001, there were 95 of these claims received by the small claims procedure, a drop of 15 fro similar claims received the previous year. A grand total of 612 other types of small claim were received by the service in each of the years, 2000 and 2001.

CLAIMS DEALT WITH

While the above represented the number and type of small claims cases received by the Small Claims procedure in those two years, the following number of cases were dealt with. The Small Claims Registrars settled a grand total of 1, 453 cases in 2001 compared with 1,611 in 2000.

The number of cases actually referred to the court in those years was 879 and 843, respectively. A further number of 283 cases were not proceeded with in 2001, 53 more than in the previous year while a further 32 cases were not covered by the small claims procedure in 2001.

In previous chapters we examined the system under which a claimant is able to get judgment by default against a respondent who fails to respond or ignores a claim taken against him. In 2001, there were 432 decrees by default granted by the court, just two more than the number of such decrees granted the previous year.

The year to March 2003: Dublin

As would be expected, the Dublin Metropolitan District Court receives the largest number of small claims. This is not only because of the population factor but because many of the companies, including travel companies and airlines against whom claims were taken by consumers living in the provinces have their offices in the capital. A good example of this is apparent from the figures shown for holidays in the list below. A total of 246 such cases were received, including claims for lost baggage and other claims relating to holidays.

In the year up to March 1st this year, a total of 1,332 cases were handled by Courts Service staff in the District Court office dedicated to small claims in Áras Uí Dhálaigh, Inns Quay, beside the Four Courts in Dublin 7. The following are the type and number of claims on the books of this office:

Type of Claim	No. of Claims
Appliance repairs	22
Bicycles	2
Building	57
Carpet/flooring	37
Children's goods	16
Clothes	53
Courses/Gym	22
Curtains	6
Doors/roofs/windows	51
Dry cleaners	69
Electrical goods	49
Entertainment	20
Furniture	94
Gardening	13
Hairdressers	2
Heating	4
Holidays	246
Insurance	10
Jewellery	15
Legal services	1
Luggage	20
Medical	8
Minor damage	21
Motor vehicles	78
Others	79
Painting & decorating	5
Photography	10
Plumbing	3
Rent deposit	154
Services	38
Shoes	26
Upholstery	3

That is a very interesting list of claims, included among are claims for children's goods such as toys, buggies and pushchairs; claims relating to faulty computers; claims arising out of dissatisfaction with concerts such as paying for a ticket and then being seated behind a pillar and claims arising out of the Santa Kingdom cancellation; a claim against a hairdresser as a result of receiving highlights which turned out a different colour than was ordered; claims relating to rings and faulty bracelets; unsatisfactory dentures and faulty medical appliances; claim for unpaid compensation after damage caused to car by other motorist and a claim by a person unhappy with their wedding photographs. The list is long and varied.

Outside Dublin

For a pin picture of how the small claims procedure is used outside Dublin, we will examine an area that extends southeast from its border with south county Dublin. The Bray District Court Area is one of the largest and also one of the busiest in the country. The area includes the District Courts of the county town of Wicklow and also of Rathdrum, high up in the Wicklow Mountains. Small claims account for a considerable number of the business handled by the Small Claims Registrar and his staff in the Bray office.

A breakdown of the claims received in 2002 in that area shows the following type and number of claims for goods and supplies, followed by the type and number of claims for services. The cases handled by the office during the year numbered a total of 83, 13 of which were on its books at the start of 2002.

Type of Claim	No. of Claims
Electrical goods	5
Audio/Hi-Fi/computer equipment	17
Clothes	2
Shoes	3
Jewellery	1
Furniture	11
Carpets/flooring	2
Doors/roofs/windows	3
Motor vehicles	10
Bicycles	2
Services:	
Medical	1
Holidays	3
Dry cleaners	1
Building	2
Plumbing	1
Painting & decorating	3
Damage to private property	1
Key money (rent deposits)	14
Detinue of goods (i.e. wrongful retention)	1

The records also show that at the end of 2002, the Bray office had 31 claims on its books, which were not listed for court. When compared with the total number on hand and then received during the year, a total of 52 claims were dealt with during the 12 months up to December 31 last.

Looking at the figures more closely, we see that two cases were not covered by the small claims procedure while a further case was not proceeded with. A total of 18 decrees in default were granted while the Registrar settled 25 cases. The court dealt with six cases. Of these six, decrees were granted in two of them, three were dismissed and one was withdrawn.

The statistics provided by the Bray office also show that they received 57 claims where the value of the claim was less than €600 and 26 cases where the value was greater than that value.

The County Registrar, as Sheriff, and her staff were also very effective in enforcing judgments sent to her office by the small claims court. Of the 18 decrees sent, a total of 12 were enforced. Only one was returned marked 'no goods.'

APPENDIX A

LEGAL WORDS AND TERMS EXPLAINED

Acceptance of liability (Notice of): When the respondent admits responsibility, fault or liability for the loss or damage claimed by the applicant. The form the respondent completes is Form 53A.3. See **Appendix B.**

Affidavit: A written statement made under oath.

Affirmation: This is a substitute for the oath and is used in cases where the person giving evidence, whether verbally or by affidavit, objects to taking the oath on the ground of religious belief or in the absence of having a religious belief. Instead, the person affirms as follows: "I AB do solemnly, sincerely and truly declare and affirm……."

Appeal: The process of asking a higher court to review the lower court's decision.

Applicant: The person making a small claim.

Application: The form the applicant uses to commence the claim.

Arbitration: One of the most common ways in which a right of bringing an action is suspended or stayed is by entering into an agreement to arbitrate upon differences that may arise. Where a person has agreed to arbitration, the courts will not permit him to bring an action on the subject of the dispute until the arbitration has been decided. Arbitration hears are conducted in private. However, holiday contracts normally contain a statement to the effect that if the claim is for a sum of money less than the maximum that the Small Claims Court can award (€1,269.74), the claimant may have the dispute decided by the Small Claims Procedure.

Claimant: The party who is making a claim.

Counterclaim: A claim by the respondent in response to the claimant's claim. It is a separate but related claim which is usually adjudicated on by the judge at the same time as the main claim. Essentially, it is a claim presented by the respondent against the claimant.

Decree: A written order made by the District Court in a small claim.

Default judgment: A judgment in favour of the claimant because the respondent failed, for example, to show up for the trial which the respondent had a duty to do.

Execution: the legal process of enforcing a judgment.

Garnishee: A third party, such as an employer or bank, who has money belonging to the losing party (e.g. the respondent). The third party is ordered to give the money to the court (for the benefit of the claimant) rather than to the losing party.

Judgment: The decision of the court.

Judgment debtor: A party who owes money to someone else according to a decision of a court.

Liability: The fault or responsibility of a party for causing for an act for which he is liable to a person who suffered loss or damage as a result.

Notice of dispute: The form completed by the respondent when dispute responsibility for the claim. It is form 53A.4. See **Appendix B.**

Oath: A form of words by which a person calls his/her God to witness what he/she is saying is the truth.

Party: One of the parties to a Small Claims Procedure. It can be either the claimant or the respondent.

Respondent: The party against whom the claim is taken.

Service: The delivery to a person of an official court document by an authorised court official or by pre-paid registered post.

Small Claims Court: It is the District Court when presiding over a small claim, i.e. one that has a current upper limit of €1,269.74. It is a people's court and was designed to help people handle their small cases without the assistance of a solicitor. The court staff are there to help a party prepare the proper papers in order to file a claim and, if the party wins, to help collect the money. People are able to engage a solicitor (and barrister) but they must discharge the legal fees from their own resources because the court does not award costs to the party that wins.

Subpoena: A written summons addressed to someone, such as a witness, ordering his or her attendance in court, if that person does not want to attend voluntarily.

APPENDIX B

FORMS

Form 53A.1

Claim No. _____

AN CHUIRT DUICHE

THE DISTRICT COURT

DUBLIN METROPOLITAN DISTRICT

District Court (Small Claims Procedure) Rules 1999, Rule 3.
APPLICATION TO SMALL CLAIMS REGISTRAR

CLAIMANT	**RESPONDENT**
Name and address of person making the claim	Name and address of person against whom the claim is made

Telephone No: _____

CLAIM: Set out particulars of the claim

Amount claimed: €

Particulars of claim:

I hereby apply to have the claim processed through the Small Claims Procedure in accordance with the provisions of the above mentioned Rules

To: *The Small Claims Registrar*
Aras Uí Dhalaigh
Inns Quay
Dublin 7
Telephone: 8886000

Dated this   day of   2003

_____
Signature of the person making the claim
Note: This application must be accompanied by a fee of €7

GUIDE TO COMPLETING YOUR APPLICATION

Please note: Due to the Volume of Claims being processed by this office it may be up to 8 weeks before you can expect any response to your claim.

1. Under the heading "Claimant" fill in your own name, address and telephone number (if any).

2. Under the heading "Respondent" fill in the name and **retail outlet address** of the person or company you are making the claim against. It is important that you have the correct title (name) of the Respondent as a Court Order cannot be enforced against an incorrect title.

The name which is over the shop or on the receipt etc. may not be sufficient. You should state either the owner's name or the name of the Limited Company which is trading under that name.

If you are unsure about this you should go to the Companies Registration Office, Parnell House, 14 Parnell Square, Dublin 1, and have a search done on the company.

3. State amount claimed. (Maximum EUR 1,269.74)

4. Give brief details of your claim stating when you purchased the goods or service, how much you paid for them and what the problem is.

5. Date and sign the form.

6. Send the form together with EUR 7.00 (Government Stamp Duty which is non-refundable) to: The Small Claims Registrar, Aras Ui Dhalaigh, Inns Quay, Dublin, 7.

Your application will be processed as soon as possible after it is received. A copy will be sent by Registered Post to the Respondent and as soon the Respondent replies a copy of the reply will be posted to you.

If the Respondent fails to reply to the claim you are entitled to Judgment by Default, provided a specific amount is claimed in your application. If after 8 weeks approx. you receive no reply from this office or from the Respondent directly you should contact this office to swear an Affidavit of Debt to obtain the judgment.

If the Respondent fails to pay as directed then the decree will be sent to the Sheriff for execution, on payment by you of his fee of EUR 7.62.

You can contact this office at 8886130/8886592/8886192

Claim No:931/20

DUBLIN METROPOLITAN DISTRICT
District Court(Small Claims Procedure) Rules 1999,Rule 11.
SMALL CLAIMS DECREE (Summary Judgement)

BETWEEN

Of: Claimant

AND

Of: and Court District aforesaid
                                                 Respondent

1. IT APPEARING that a Notice of claims was duly served on the Respondent(s) claiming €

2. That the Respondent failed to return Form 53A.3/53A.4 to the Small Claims Registrar
3. AND IT FURTHER APPEARING by the affidavit of the Claimant verifying the said claim, Sworn
the **10th day of December 2002** and the request for judgement thereon that the Respondent(s)
Is/are justly indebted to the Claimant in the sum of €

IT IS THEREFORE ORDERED AND DECREED that the Claimant(s) do recover from the Respondent(s)
Said sum of € in satisfaction of the said debt ,and all the sheriffs and county registrars are hereby
commanded to take in execution the goods of the Respondent to satisfy the said debt.

Dated at Dublin this   day of   2003

                              Signed_____
                              Judge of the District Court

                              Signed_____
                              Small Claims Registrar
                              Of Aras Ui Dhalaigh, Inns Quay,Dublin 7

County of   I authorise and Empower

           To WIT   of

_____
And   of

Court Messengers, or either of them, and their Assistants, to execute the above Decree.
The sum to be levied hereunder is €

Dated the   day of   2003

                    _____
                    Sheriff or Co Registrar for the said County

Claim No:

DUBLIN METROPOLITAN DISTRICT
District Court(Small Claims Procedure) Rules 1999, rule 9 & 13
SMALL CLAIMS DECREE

Of:

Claimant

AND

Of:

And Court   District Aforesaid
Respondent

Was served on the Respondent .And the small Claims Registrar having failed to settle the claim, has
Entered it for hearing by the court on 2/01/03 and has notified both parties accordingly. And it further appearing that
the Respondent is justly indebted to the Claimant in the sum of €
It is therefore Ordered and Decreed by the Judge that the Claimant do recover from the Respondent
The sum of €, and all the several Sheriffs and County Registrars acting as such in Ireland are
Hereby commanded to take in execution the GOODS of the Respondent, to satisfy the said Debt.

Dated at Dublin this   day of   2003

                              Signed_____
                              Judge of the District Court

                              Signed_____
                              Small Claims Registrar
                              Of Aras Ui Dhalaigh, Inns Quay,Dublin 7

County of   I authorise and Empower

         To WIT   of

And   of
Court Messengers, or either of them, and their Assistants, to execute the above Decree.
The sum to be levied hereunder is €

Dated the   day of   2003

                      _____
                      Sheriff or Co. Registrar for the said County

Claim No. _____

AN CHUIRT DUICHE   **THE DISTRICT COURT**

DUBLIN METROPOLITAN DISTRICT
District Court (Small Claims Procedure) Rules 1999, Rule 11.

AFFIDAVIT OF DEBT

Between   Claimant

AND

                                                              Respondent

I,

aged 18 years and upwards make oath and say as follows:-

1.   I am the Claimant herein and I am duly authorised to make this affidavit. The facts herein stated are within my own knowledge save where otherwise appears.

2.   I am informed and believe that

      (a) the notice claiming the sum of €   was served on the Respondent on the
                 day of   2003.
      (b) Form 53A.3/53A.4 admitting or disputing the claim has not been received by the Small Claims Registrar from the Respondent.

      (c) the claim has been settled for the sum of
         but the agreed terms thereof have not been complied with by the Respondent.

3.   No sum whatever/the sum of   , only has been paid on foot of this claim and the sum of   is now actually due and owing to me by the Respondent, and I now request judgment against him in this amount.

Sworn before me at
             in the County of the
City of Dublin this   day
of   2003
and I know the Deponent.

_____   _____
Deponent   Small Claims Registrar

Claim No:

Form 53A.2

DUBLIN METROPOLITAN DISTRICT

District Court (Small Claims Procedure) Rules, 1999. Order 53A Rule 5

NOTICE OF CLAIM AGAINST RESPONDENT

Claimant   Respondent

In said Court District.

A copy of the claim (Form 53A.1) is attached.

IF YOU ADMIT THE CLAIM, you should complete and detach Form 53A.3 and return it to the Small Claims Registrar within 15 days of receipt of this notice.

IF YOU DISPUTE THE CLAIM, you should complete and detach Form 53A.4 and return it to the Small Claims Registrar within 15 days of receipt of this notice.

IF YOU WISH TO DISCUSS THE CLAIM, with the Small Claims Registrar you should contact him/her at the address below within 15 days of receipt of this notice.

IF YOU DO NOTHING ABOUT THIS NOTICE YOU WILL BE HELD TO HAVE ADMITTED THE CLAIM AND THE CLAIMANT MAY PROCEED TO OBTAIN JUDGMENT AGAINST YOU WITHOUT FURTHER NOTICE TO YOU.

Dated:28/02/03

Small Claims Registrar
District Court Office,
Aras Ui Dhalaigh,
Four Courts, Dublin 7.
Tel: 01-8886000.

Claim No:

Form 53A.3

DUBLIN METROPOLITAN DISTRICT

District Court (Small Claims Procedure) Rules, 1999. Order 53A rule

NOTICE OF ACCEPTANCE OF LIABILITY

Claimant   Respondent

I admit the claim made against me in the above matter and

* I agree to pay the amount claimed and enclose
  herewith cheque/postal order/money order made
  payable to the claimant, for the sum of _____
  in full settlement.

* I consent to judgment being given against me.

* I agree to pay the amount claimed and I will
  refund the full amount to the claimant when
  the goods are returned by the claimant.

* Delete clauses which   Dated this   day of   20
  do not apply.

_____
Signature of the Respondent.

To
The Small Claims Registrar,
District Court Office,
Aras Ui Dhalaigh
Four Courts,
Dublin 7. Tel 8886000.

Claim No:

DUBLIN METROPOLITAN DISTRICT

Form 53A.4

District Court (Small Claims Procedure) Rules, 1999. Order 53A rule 13

NOTICE OF DISPUTE OF CLAIM

Claimant   Respondent

* I deny the claim made against me in the above matter for the following
  reasons:-

* I wish to counterclaim for the sum of   for the following reasons.

WHERE A COUNTERCLAIM IS MADE THIS NOTICE MUST BE ACCOMPANIED BY
A FEE OF 7.00 Euro.
*DELETE CLAUSES WHICH DO NOT APPLY.

                              Dated this   day of   2003

to The Small Claims Registrar
   District Court Office
   Aras Ui Dhalaigh,
   Four Courts,   _____
   Dublin 7.   Signature of the Respondent.
   01 8886000
Note
Rule 13. The claimant and the respondent shall be liable for their own
legal costs and witnesses expenses (if any) incurred under the Small
Claims Procedure.

APPENDIX C

LIST OF DISTRICT COURT OFFICE ADDRESSES

CARLOW

Carlow Address:	**Chief Clerk:** William F. Dunphy, District Court Office, The Court House, Court Place, Carlow, Co. Carlow **Tel:** (0503) 31225. **Fax:** (0503) 31325 Office hours: Mon-Fri - 10am-12.30pm 2.30pm-4.30pm **Also** White's Hotel, George St., Wexford. **Tel:** (053) 22311. **Also** Ferrycarrig Hotel, Ferrycarrig Bridge, Wexford. **Tel:** (053) 20999.
Athy Office	same as Carlow
Baltinglass	,,
Muine Bheag	,,
Tullow	,,

CAVAN

Cavan Address:	**Chief Clerk:** Noel Brennan, District Court Office, The Court House Farnham Street, Cavan, Co Cavan. **Tel:** (049) 4331585 **Fax:** (049) 4331590 Office hours: Mon - Fri - 9.15am - 1pm 2pm - 5pm
Arva Office	same as Cavan
Bailieborough	,,
Ballyconnell and	,,
Ballyjamesduff	,,
Belturbet	,,
Cootehill	,,
Kingscourt	,,
Oldcastle	,,
Swanlinbar	,,
Virginia	,,

CLARE

Ennis	**Chief Clerk:** Josephine Tone,
Address:	District Court Office,
	1 Bindon Street, Ennis, Co.Clare.
	Tel: (065) 6821682. **Fax:** (065) 6821908
Corofin Office	same as Ennis
Ennistymon	,,
Kidysart	,,
Kilkee	,,
Killaloe	,,
Kilrush	,,
Lisdoonvarna	,,
Miltown Malbay	,,
Shannon	,,
Tulla	,,

CORK

Cork	**Chief Clerk:** Finbarr Bracken,
Address:	District Court Office,
	The Court House,
	Anglesea Street," Cork.
	Tel: (021) 4319610. **Fax:** (021) 4319614
Coachford Office	same as Cork
Cobh	,,
Cork City	,,
Kinsale	,,

Clonakilty	**Chief Clerk:** Denis Noonan,
Address:	The Court House,
	Lamb Street, Clonakilty, Co. Cork.
	Tel: (023) 35759 **Fax:** (023) 35767
Bantry Office	same as Clonakilty
Dunmanway	,,
Glengarriff	,,
Macroom	,,
Schull	,,
Skibereen	,,
Fermoy	**Chief Clerk:** Tom Browne,
Address:	District Court Office,
	Mill Island,
	Fermoy, Co. Cork.
	Tel: (025) 31160. **Fax:** (025) 33656

Lismore Office	same as Fermoy
Mitchelstown	,,
Tallow	,,
Mallow Chief Clerk:	Michael McEvoy.
Address:	District Court Office,
	The Court House,
	O'Brien Street, Mallow, Co. Cork
	Tel: (022) 21486. **Fax:** (022) 21249
Drumcollogher Office	same as Mallow
Kanturk	,,
Millstreet	,,
Youghal Chief Clerk:	Marian Beiti Byrne.
Address:	District Court Office,
	The Court House,
	Town Hall (Parallel with Main Street),
	Youghal, Co. Cork.
	Tel: (024) 92175. **Fax:** (024) 92889
Dungarvan Office	same as Youghal
Middleton	,,

DONEGAL

Letterkenny	**Chief Clerk:** Val Cronin.
Address:	District Court Office,
	The Court House,
	Main Street, Letterkenny, Co. Donegal.
	Tel: (074) 21909. **Fax:** (074) 26613
Buncrana Office	same as Letterkenny
Carndonagh	,,
Falcarragh	,,
Donegal	**Chief Clerk:** Daniel O'Grady,
Address:	District Court Office,
	The Court House,
	Main Street, Donegal.
	Tel: (073) 21532. **Fax:** (073) 21947
Ballyshannon Office	same as Donegal
Dungloe	,,
Glenties	,,

GALWAY

Ballinasloe	**Chief Clerk:** Patricia Mulkerrin.
Address:	District Court Office,
	The Court House,
	Ballinasloe, Co. Galway
	Tel: (0905) 42342. **Fax:** (0905) 44731.
Ballyforan Office	same as Ballinasloe

Banagher   same as Ballinasloe
Eyrecourt   ,,
Glenamaddy   ,,
Mountbellew   ,,
Loughrea Chief Clerk: Brendan McDonald.
Address: District Court Office,
                          The Court House,
                          The Green, Loughrea, Co. Galway.
                          Tel: (091) 841463 **Fax:** (091) 847272
Borrisokane Office   same as Loughrea
Portumna   ,,
Scarriff   ,,
Galway   **Chief Clerk:** Peter Raftery.
                          "Delores Gordon (Small Claims)."
Address: District Court House,
                          The Court House,
                          (Opposite Francis Street), Galway.
                          Tel: (091) 562560. **Fax:** (091) 564895
Athenry Office   same as Galway
Gort   ,,
Headfort   ,,
Kinvara   ,,
Derrynea   **Chief Clerk:** John Browne,
Address: District Court Office,
                          The Court House,
                          Derrynea, Costelloe, Co. Galway.
                          Tel: (091) 572202. **Fax:** (091) 572078
Carna Office   same as Derrynea
Clifden   ,,
Kilronan   ,,
Kilronan   ,,
Letterfrack   ,,
Maam   ,,
Oughterard   ,,
Spiddal   ,,
Tuam Chief Clerk: Patrick M.S. Murphy.
Address: District Court Office,
                          The Shambles,
                          Vicar Street, Tuam, Co. Galway.
                          Tel: (093) 24318. **Fax:** (093) 70234
Ballinrobe Office   same as Tuam
Dunmore   ,,
Derreen   ,,
Ballyhaunis   ,,

KERRY

Killarney	**Chief Clerk:** M.A. Mac Amhlaoi,
Address:	Distrist Court Office,
	Rushbrooke House,
	Upper Lewis Road, Killarney, Co. Kerry.
	Tel: (064) 31142. **Fax:** (064) 30233
Cahirciveen office	same as Killarney
Castletown Bere	,,
Kenmare	,,
Killorglin	,,
Sneem	,,
Waterville	,,
Listowel Chief Clerk:	Peter Cotter.
Address:	District Court Office,
	The Court House,
	(Off Charles Street),
	Listowel, Co. Kerry.
	Tel: (068) 21220. **Fax:** (068) 23825
Abbeyfeale Office	same as Listowel
Newcastlewest	,,
Tralee Chief Clerk:	Richard Maguire.
Address:	District Court Office,
	The Court House,
	Ashe Street, Tralee, Co. Kerry.
	Tel: (066) 7121187. **Fax:** (066) 7180250
Annascaul Office	same as Tralee
Castlegregory	,,
Castleisland	,,
Dingle	,,

KILDARE

Naas Chief Clerk:	Cornelius Delahunty.
Address:	District Court Office,
	The Court House,
	Main Street, Naas, Co. Kildare.
	Tel: (045) 897430. **Fax:** (045) 866731
Droichead Nua Office	same as Naas
Dunlavin	,,
Kilcock	,,
Kildare	,,

KILKENNY

Kilkenny	**Chief Clerk:** Bernard Byrne.
Address:	District Court Office,
	The Court House,
	Parliament Street, Kilkenny.
	Tel: (056) 21019. **Fax:** (056) 23260
Callan	ame as Kilkenny
Thomastown	,,
Urlingford Office	,,

LAOIS

Portlaoise Chief Clerk: John Purcell.	
Address:	Courthouse,
	Main Street, Portlaoise, Co. Laois.
	Tel: (0502) 21158. **Fax:** (0502) 20828
Castlecomer Office	same as Portlaoise
Portarlington	,,
Rathdowney	,,

LETRIM

Carrick-on-Shannon	**Chief Clerk:** Leo Mulvey.
Address:	District Court Office,
	The (New) Court House,
	(Back of Garda Station),
	Carrick-on-Shannon, Co. Leitrim.
	Tel: (078) 20481 **Fax:** (078) 22061
	Office hours: Mon - Fri - 10am - 1pm
	2pm - 4pm
Ballinamore Office	same as Carrick-on-Shannon
Ballyfarnon	,,
Boyle	,,
Dowra	,,
Drumkerrin	,,

LIMERICK

Limerick Chief Clerk: J.V. Woods.	
	District Court Office,
	The Court House,
	Merchant's Quay, Limerick.
	Tel: (061) 414300 **Fax:** (061) 414926
Adare Office	same as Limerick
Bruff	,,
Kilmallock	,,

Newport	same as Limerick
Rathkeale	,,
Shanagolden	,,

LONGFORD

Longford Chief Clerk: Michael Walsh.
Address: District Court Office,
Church Street, Longford.
Tel: (043) 46491 **Fax:** (043) 45449

Granard Office same as Longford

LOUTH

Drogheda **Chief Clerk:** P. Ó Duinn,
Address: District Court Office,
The Old Library,
Fair Street, Drogheda, Co. Louth.
Tel: (041) 9838313. **Fax:** (041) 9836297

Dunleer Office same as Drogheda
Dundalk **Chief Clerk:** Daniel Doyle,
Address: District Court Office,
The Court House,
The Ramparts, Dundalk, Co. Louth.
Tel: (042) 4334343 **Fax:** (042) 9334698

Ardee Office same as Dundalk
Carlingford ,,

MAYO

Ballina **Chief Clerk:** Siobhán Terry.
Address: District Court Office,
The Court House,
Francis Street, Ballina, Co. Mayo.
Tel: (096) 72940. **Fax:** (096) 72944

Ballycastle same as Ballina
Ballycroy ,,
Belmullet ,,
Easky ,,
Foxford ,,
Inniscrone ,,
Swinford ,,
Castlebar **Chief Clerk:** John Healy.
Address: District Court Office,
The Court House,
Spencer Street, Castlebar, Co. Mayo.

Tel: (094) 21764 **Fax:** (094) 21990
Office hours:
Mon-Thu: 9.15am - 1pm. 2.15pm - 5.30pm
Friday: 9.15am - 1pm, 2.15pm - 5.15pm

Achill Office	same as Castlebar
Claremorris	,,
Kiltimagh	,,
Westport	,,

MEATH

Trim Chief Clerk: Timothy McCarthy.
Address: District Court Office,
The Court House,
Trim, Co. Meath.
Tel: (046) 31360. **Fax:** (046) 31794

Dunshaughlin Office	same as Trim
Navan	,,
Ceanannus Mór	,,

MONAGHAN

Monaghan **Chief Clerk:** Brendan Cleary,
Address: District Court Office,
The Court House,
Church Square, Monaghan.
Tel: (047) 81417. **Fax:** (047) 81542

Ballybay Office	same as Monaghan
Carrickmacross	,,
Castleblayney	,,
Clones	,,

OFFALY

Tullamore Chief Clerk: Denis O'Leary
Address: District Court Office,
The Court House,
Cormac Street, Tullamore, Co. Offaly.
Tel: (0506) 21153. **Fax:** (0506) 21626

Edenderry Office	same as Tullamore

ROSCOMMON

Roscommon Chief Clerk: Aidan Cashin.
Address: District Court Office,
                      The Court House,
                      Abbey Street, Roscommon.
                      Tel: (0903) 26174. **Fax:** (0903) 25833
                      Ballaghderreen Office   same as Roscommon
Castlerea   ,,
Elphin   ,,
Mohill   ,,
Rooskey   ,,
Strokestown   ,,
Williamstown   ,,

SLIGO

Sligo Chief Clerk: William Cashell.
Address: District Court Office,
                      The Court House,
                      Teeling Street, Sligo.
                      Tel: (071) 42429. **Fax:** (071) 42297
Ballymote Office   same as Sligo
Charlestown   ,,
Collooney   ,,
Grange   ,,
Manorhamilton   ,,
Riverstown   ,,
Skreen   ,,
Tubbercurry   ,,

TIPPERARY

Clonmel   **Chief Clerk:** Michael Goulding,
Address: District Court Office,
                      The Court House,
                      Nelson Street, Clonmel, Co. Tipperary.
                      Tel: (052) 29220 **Fax:** (052) 28699
                      Office hours:
                      Mon-Thur: 9.15am-1pm, 2.15pm - 5.30pm
                      Friday: 9.15am - 1pm, 2.15pm - 5.15pm"
Cahir Office   same as Clonmel
Cappoquin   ,,
Cashel   ,,
Killenaule   ,,
Tipperary   ,,

Nenagh Chief Clerk: John Buckley.
Address: District Court Office,
                           Friar Court,
                           Abbey Street, Nenagh, Co. Tipperary.
                           Tel: (067) 31319. **Fax:** (067) 41405
Birr Office   same as Nenagh
Thurles Chief Clerk: Martin Hanton.
Address: District Court Office,
                           2 Parnell Street,
                           Thurles," Co. Tipperary.
                           Tel: (0504) 21343. **Fax:** (0504) 22289
Roscrea Office   same as Thurles
Templemore   ,,

WATERFORD
Waterford Chief Clerk: Thomas A. Treanor.
Address: District Court Office,
                           The Court House,
                           Catherine Street, Waterford.
                           Tel: (051) 874657. **Fax:** (051) 876852
Carrick-on-Suir Office same as Waterford
Kilmacthomas   ,,

WESTMEATH
Athlone   **Chief Clerk**: Martin Conlon
Address: District Court Office,
                           The Court House,
                           Pearse Street, Athlone, Co. Westmeath
                           Tel: (0902) 92271. **Fax:** (0902) 93385
Kilcormac Office   same as Athlone
Moate   ,,
Mullingar   **Chief Clerk:** Patrick Kelly.
Address: District Court Office,
                           The Court House,
                           Mount Street, Mullingar, Co. Westmeath.
Tel: (044) 48364. **Fax:** (044) 48716
Castlepollard Office   same as Mullingar
Killucan   ,,

WEXFORD

Gorey	**Chief Clerk:** William Sexton.
Address:	District Court Office,
	The Court House,
	(Opposite Garda Station),
	Gorey, Co. Wexford.
Tel:	(055) 21379. **Fax:** (055) 22177
Arklow Office	same as Gorey
Wexford Chief Clerk:	Patrick Looney.
Address:	District Court Office,
	County Hall,
	Hill Street, Wexford.
Tel:	(053) 22097. **Fax:** (053) 24798
Enniscorthy Office	same as Wexford
New Ross	,,

WICKLOW

Bray	**Chief Clerk:** Alan Donnellan.
Address:	District Court Office,
	The Court House,
	Boghall Road, Bray, Co. Wicklow.
	Tel: (01) 2862474 **Fax:** (01) 2869985
Rathdrum Office	same as Bray
Wicklow	**County Registrar:** Breda Allen
Address:	Courthouse, Wicklow
Tel:	(0404) 67361 **Fax:** (0404) 67422
Office hours:	9:15am-5:30pm
	Parking facilities: Street parking at present
Public phones:	Yes
Public toilets:	Yes
Transportation: Train:	Dublin – Arklow – Rosslare Harbour
Bus:	Dublin - Rosslare Harbour Route.
	Dublin - Arklow Route.
Accommodation:	The Grand Hotel.
Address:	Abbey Street, Wicklow.
Tel:	(0404) 67337.
Also	The Bayview Hotel, The Mall, Wicklow.
Tel:	(0404) 67383.

APPENDIX D

SMALL CLAIMS COURT SITTINGS IN 2003

The following are the dates on which the Small Claims Court is scheduled to sit in Dublin for the remainder of this year (2003):

June 4, 11, 18, 25.

July 9, 16, 23, 30.

No sittings will take place during the month of August.

September 3, 10, 17, 24.

October 1, 8, 15, 22, 29.

November, 5, 12, 19, 26.

December, 3, 10, 17.

The hearings are held in court number 54 in the Richmond Buildings. The court sits between 10.30am and 1pm when it closes for lunch. The court resumes at 2pm and continues until 4pm.

INDEX

Acceptance of liability (Notice of)
definition of, 83
form 43A.3, 27
Affidavit, 2, 29, *see also*
Affidavit of debt and Oath
definition of, 83
Affidavit of debt,
definition of, 28,
drafting of, 28
lodgment of, 28, 34
swearing of, 34
Affirmation, 2, 44, 54, *see also*
Evidence and Oath
definition of, 83
Alternative dispute resolution (ADR), 63, *see also*
Arbitration
Appeal, 38, 61, 64, 65
Circuit Court to, 38, 46, 47,
48, 52, 70
circumstances of taking, 48
costs of, 46
court of final appeal, 9
courts, 12
definition of, 83
European Member States in,
64, 65
excluded right to, 61, 65
grounds for, 47
notice of, 48
restrictions on right to, 61
right of, 8, 70
Applicant,
definition of, 83
notice of application, 26
Application, *see also* **Small Claims**
adjournment of, 43
granting of, 43

original, 37
notice of,
form 53A.1, 24, 26
referral of for hearing, 37
Arbitration, 76, *see also*
Alternative dispute resolution
Chartered Institute of
Arbitrators,
definition of, 83
rules of, 76
Audio and Computer Equipment,
claims for, 77, 81
Austria,
claims in, 61, 62, 63, 65
Bailiff, 47, 51
Barrister, 8, 39, 40, 43, *see also*
Solicitor
costs of, 48, 85, *see also* **Fees**
representation by, 3, 10, 46,
48, 85
Belgium,
claims in, 61, 63
Bray District Court Area,
claims in, 51, 80, 81, 82
Builders,
Claims relating to, 77, 79, 81
Carpets, *see also* **Floor Coverings**
damage to, 20, 21, 77, 79, 81
Cars, *see also* **Garage**
damage to, 80
defective, 72, 73, 74, 77
Case histories, 66-74
Charging orders, 56
Children's goods,
Claims relating to, 79, 80
Circuit Court, *see also* **Appeal and Courts**

appeal, 38, 46, 47, 48, 52, 70,
    see **Appeal**
award of damages by, 9
decree by judge of, 36
default procedure in, 34
representation in, 10, *see*
    Barrister and **Solicitor**
rules for, 9
trial in, 9
Citizen's Information Centres,
    22
Civil proceedings, 1, 3,
    Hearing of, 34, 35
Claim, *see* **Small Claims**
    Civil, 8-14
Claimant,
    body corporate as, 2
    complaint by, letter of, 20, 21
    definition of, 1
    pro, 3
Clothes,
Claims relating to, 79, 81
Commission of the European
    Union,
    Green Paper of, 58
    Member States, monetary
        limits in, 61, 62
Companies Registration Office,
    24
Concert,
    Claims relating to, 80
Constitution, 4, 7, 9, 12
Consumer,
    communication, 17
    contracts and, 15
    definition, 1
    duties of, 17, 18
    mitigate loss, 17
    expectations of, 15, 16
    pre-condition to claim by, 17
    rights of, 15, 16
    unspoken contracts, 15
Costs, 18, 34, 40, 46, 48, 55,

    59, 76, 85, *see also* **Fees**
European Member States in,
    64
    Contract, 15-17
    holiday, 83
    mitigation of loss, 17, 18
    terms of, 15
    unspoken, 15
Counterclaim, 31, 36, 40, 42,
    46, 53, *see also* **Small Claims**
    definition, 35, 84
Courts Service, viii, 78
    Guide for Small Claims, 3
    website of, 22
Courts, 9, *see also* **Civil**
    Proceedings, District Court,
    Circuit Court, High Court,
    Small Claims Court and
    Supreme Court
Cross-border Disputes, 59, 76

Damages (Award of),
    barred from claiming, 2
    jurisdiction, 8
    limits in courts, 9,18, *see*
        Limits (Damages of)
    personal injuries for, 2, 25
Decree, 28, 31, 34, 35, 36, 46,
    48, 50, 75, 82
    collection rates, 50
    default by, 78, 81
    definition, 84
    District Court rules, 53
    enforcement of, 2, 19, 46, 51,
        55
    examples of, 68, 70, 71, 72,
        73
    execution of, *see* **Execution of**
        decree
    garnishee, 56, 57, *see*
        Garnishee
    limit on amounts awarded in,
        9, 46

payment by instalments, 55
recovery of, 19
setting aside of, 35, 36,37, 38, 66
   sheriff and, 49, 50, 52
unpaid, 52, 53
Wicklow, County in, 51
Default judgment,
definition of, 84
Denmark,
claims in, 61
Deterrent, 57
Director of Consumer Affairs,
Office of, 22
District Court, 1, 3, 5, 9, *see also* **Small Claims Court**
award of damages by, 9, *see also* **Damages**
clerk, *see* **District Court Clerk**
Dublin, 4
list of, 5,
trial in, 9
District Court Clerk, 2, 5, 6, 13, *see also* **small claims registrar**
functions of, 6
negotiation of settlement by, 13
power of, 2
Drycleaners,
claims relating to, 50, 79, 81
Dublin Metropolitan Area, 22, 78-80

Electrical goods, 77, 79, 81
Enforcement of judgments, 53, *see* **Judgment**
England,
claims in, 2, 61, 62, 63, 64
Evidence, 21, 41, 44, 45, 54, 61, 65
affirmation, *see* **Affirmation**

conclusion, 45
conflict of, 8
cross-examination, 10, 44, 45
direct, 10, 44, 67
documentary, 44, 45, 63
expert, 42
giving, 10, 11, 13, 19, 45, 83
in-chief, 10, 44
inferences for, 12
oath, *see* **Oath**
rules of, 63, 64
transcript of, 12
types of, 41
veracity of, 12
witnesses, *see* **Witnesses**
Execution of decrees, 49, *see also* **Decree**
definition of, 48, 84

Farming community, 36
Fees, *see also* **Costs**
claims', 22, 23
lawyers', 18, 40, 85
Finland,
claims in, 61
Floor coverings, *see also* **Carpets**
claims for, 78, 81
defective, 37, 77
France,
claims in, 60, 61, 62, 63, 64
Furniture,
claims for, 77, 79, 81
damage to, 68

Garage, *see also* **Cars**
Claims against, 73, 74
Garnishee, 57, *see also* **Decree**
definition, 56, 84
Germany,
claims in, 60, 61, 62, 63, 64, 65
Greece
claims in, 60, 63

Hairdressers,
claims against, 79, 80
Hearing
calling of case, 43, 44
evidence, 44, 45
guidelines, 42
judgment, 45, 46
preparation for, 40
witnesses, 41, 42
High Court, 12, *see also* **Courts**
defamation case in, 12
full jurisdiction of, 9
judgment in default
procedure, 34
master of, 36
Northern Ireland, 64
power to award unlimited
damages, 9
preparation for hearing in, 40
set-aside, 36, *see also* **Set-aside**
settlement of cases in, 43
Hire purchase,
agreements, 1, 19, 25
Holiday,
accidents on, 59
claims, 75, 76, 78, 79, 81
contracts, 83
insurance, 72
Hotels,
owner, 59
claims against, 76

Instalment orders, 52, 53, 55, 56
procedure for, 29, 30, 31
Internet,
application forms, 22
ordering goods on, 59
Insurance claims, 79,
Ireland,
claims in, 5, 7, 60- 64
Italy,
claims in, 60, 63

Jewellery shop
claims against, 66, 67, 68, 79, 81
Judge, 8, 11-13, *see also* **Small Claims Court**
Judgment, 35, 36, 45, 46, 47, *see also* **Small Claims Court**
appeals against, 64, 65, *see also* **Appeal**
default, 79, 84
definition of, 84
enforcement, 52, 53, 55, 56, 82, *see also* **Execution of decrees**
in default procedure, 34
requisition for by claimant, 34
respondent consenting to, 28, 31, 34
set-aside, *see* set-aside
summary judgment form, 49,
Judgment debtor, 57
definition of, 84

Leasing agreements,
breach of, 1, 19, 25
Liability, 45
definition of, 84
notice of acceptance of, 27, 33, 83
Limits (awards of damages), 2, 3, 66
Circuit Court, 9
District Court in, 2, 3, 6, 7, 9
High Court in, 9
Monetary in Member States of EU, 61, 62
Small claims Court, 9, 85
Lost baggage,
claims for, 72, 78
Luxembourg
claims in, 61
Minister for Justice
intervention by, 56

Mitigation, 17
fundamental principle of
contract law, 17

Negligence, 2
Netherlands, The,
claims in, 61
Northern Ireland,
claims in, 2, 60, 61, 62, 64
Notice of Dispute, 33, 44
definition of, 84

Oath, *see also* **Affirmation,**
Evidence and Witnesses
affidavit, 83, *see also* **Affidavit**
definition of, 84
direct evidence under, 67
examination under, 53, 54
taking of, 44, 66

Portugal,
claims in, 61
Prison, 54, 55, 56
period in, 55
Procedure, 1-7, *see also* **Small**
Claims
days for hearing, 4
getting parties to meet, 32, 33
processing claim, 3-5
rules for, 1-3
Professional services,
claims against, 77
Purchaser, 1, *see* **Consumer**

Rent deposits, 76, 77, *see also*
Tenancies
claims for on-return of, 2, 25,
68, 69, 70, 71, 72, 79, 81
Respondent,
admittance of claim by, 27,
28, 31
consents to judgment, 28
definition of, 1

ignoring of claims by, 33, 34
options of, 26, 27
payment by, 29, *see also*
Instalment orders
instalments, 29, 30, 31

Scotland,
claims in, 60, 61, 62, 63, 64
Set aside, 36- 38
Settling claims, 6, 7, 13, 14,
16, 31- 33, 36- 38, 43, 63,
67, *see also* **Alternative**
dispute resolution, claims
and Arbitration
Sheriff, 47-51, 52
execution of court order by,
48
collection rate, 50
face to face confrontation, 51
fee, 48, 49
fieri facias, 49
fixtures,
dry cleaning dryers, 50
functions of, 48
leased good, 49
local, 48
practice by, 50, 51
seizure of goods by, 49, 50
Shoes,
claims relating to purchase of,
77, 79, 81
Shopping trip abroad
accident on
Small claims, *see also* **Small**
Claims Court
application, *see* **Application**
complaint, draft letter of, 20,
21
counterclaim, *see*
Counterclaim
definition, 1, 2
details of, 25, 26
disputing claims, 31-38, *see*

also **Appeal**
filing of, 24
guidelines for, 42, 43
fees for making, 22, 23
forms for, 24, 26
details on, 24, 25
Form 53A.1, 24, 26
Form 53A.2, 26
Form 53A.3, 26, 27, 33
Form 53A.4, 26, 27, 33
limits, 2, *see also* **Limits**
persons barred from making, 2
procedure for, 3-7, 17, 18-23,
   see also **Procedure** and
   Respondent
processing, 4, 5
rules for, 1, 2
settling, *see* **Settling of**
   Claims

Small Claims Court, *see also*
   Courts and District Court
award of damages by, 9, *see*
   also **Limits**
hearing in, 39-46
calling of case, 43, 44
evidence, *see Evidence*
judgment, *see* **Judgment**
preparation of case for, 40, 41
witnesses, *see* **Witnesses**
judge in, 12, 13, *see also* Judge
appointment of, 12
experience of, 13
Small Claims Registrar, 2, 5,
   13, 24, 29- 33, 35, 36, 41,
   43, *see also* **District Court**
Clerk
discretion of, 32
drafting affidavits, 28, *see also*
   Affidavit
functions of, 6, *see also*
   Settling claims
lodging forms and fees with,

22, 23, 26, 27, 33
obligations of, 25
personal contact with, 21
recoding of claimant's details
   by, 24
settling claims, 32, 33, *see also*
   Settling claims
sheriff and, 49, *see also* **Sheriff**
Solicitor, *see also* **Barrister**
fees, *see* **Fees**
leasing agreement drawn up
   by, 69
representation by, 3, 4, 5, 10,
   85

Spain,
claims in, 60, 61, 62, 63, 64
Stock and shares, attachment
   of, 56, 57
Subpoena, 41, *see also*
   Witnesses
definition of, 85
Supreme Court, 9, 12, *see also*
   Courts
Sweden,
claims in, 60, 61, 62, 63, 64

Tenancies, 2, 71, 72, *see also*
   Rent deposits
claim against landlord, 2
key money, 2
rent deposit, non-return of, 2,
   68, 76, 77
Torts, 2
negligence, 2
Trial, 9-11, 39-46, *see also*
   Courts and Small Claims
Court
judge, 11, 12, *see also* **Judge**
procedure in, 9-11

United States of America,
claims in, 2

Vendor(seller), 1, 25
  obligations of, 17

Wales,
  claims in, 60, 61, 62, 63, 64
Wicklow, County,
  claims in, 51, 80

Witnesses, 10, 11, 13, 19, 41, 42, 44, 45, 67, 71, *see also* **Affirmation, Evidence and Oath**
  expert, 41
  subpoena to, 41, 85
  voluntary attendance of, 41